For my Mum and fellow beginner gardeners

Petal Power

JULIA ATKINSON-DUNN

KOA PRESS

Published in 2021 by Koa Press Limited.

www.koapress.co.nz

Director: Tonia Shuttleworth
Editor: Lucinda Diack
Sub-editor: Belinda O'Keefe
Designer: Tonia Shuttleworth
Photographer: Julia Atkinson-Dunn

ISBN 978-0-473-55934-2

Printed in Christchurch, New Zealand by Ovato Print

All attempts were made to contact the copyright holders of the quotes and excerpts used in this book, and Julia Atkinson-Dunn would like to thank and acknowledge the authors and publishers of these words.

Left: A wild, early summer bunch from my garden featuring a delphinium, phlomis, sweet pea blooms and vine, fennel, *Verbena bonariensis*, *Verbena rigida*, *Knautia macedonica*, lobelia, forget-me-nots, cornflowers, love-in-a-mist, clematis and foraged roadside buttercups.
Front cover: Home-grown Iceland poppy, geum, nemesia, foxgloves, snapdragons, fennel and thalictrum foliage with roadside buttercups and a single peony grown by my cousins, The Peony People.

Contents

Foreword

Julia and I became firm friends over my inability with social media! I recognise her as a leader in the next generation of true gardeners. Her enthusiasm and undoubted knowledge have led her to create this enchanting book. I have watched her ability in staging art exhibitions in her own home and turning a small garden space into a huge source of interest and productivity. Her delightful enthusiasm is infectious and 'can-do' attitude only to be admired. After careful research she has created a book that will be loved and enjoyed by all generations of gardeners. This book is full of practical advice which will impart enthusiasm in all who read it.

Julia is a talented writer, clever with a camera, and her flower arrangements have a simple spontaneity which are easy to follow. The plants she has chosen to be in this book create an ethereal airiness in gardens, which is the opposite of the more structured gardens so popular in New Zealand at present. The more naturalistic approach is the way of the future and being able to pick flowers for your home or friends is a therapy like no other. Flowers are soothing and bring us all joy in every season.

Julia's little tips on growing from seed will be treasured by all who are interested in beginning a new garden or revamping an older one, at whatever stage in life. The summaries on each of her 12 favourite plants show a deep and natural understanding of the plant world. What is so wonderful about gardening is that no two years are the same, nothing is static and growing plants change in dimension all the time. It is an art form, always considering colour, form and texture. Julia connects with that so well.

Creativity is so important for us all. 'Do one creative thing every day – it will feed your soul' was my mother's gift to me and I feel sure *Petal Power* will help others along that road.

PENNY ZINO
FLAXMERE GARDEN
NZGT 6-STAR GARDEN OF INTERNATIONAL SIGNIFICANCE

Above: A casual collection of summer flowering blooms from the garden including pink and white echinacea, scabiosa, dahlias, Queen Anne's lace, marjoram, lupins and astrantia.

Let's begin

Gardening is really a bit like baking. Everyone catches whispers of tips on how to 'do it right' and 'do it best' but ultimately it's mixing the standard ingredients, crossing your fingers and hoping the result is like the picture on the packet.

What I've discovered is that it's not nearly as complicated as I thought as a non-gardener. There are only so many ways to get a plant to grow and most will win or fail with no explanation. I've learnt that gardening gets easier with each season, each mistake and each opening bloom, but most importantly that the process is surprisingly as pleasurable as the result.

For me that is the power of petals.

Consider this book your cheerleader. Offering you a smile and steadying words to help you plot your own gardening adventure. Be it full of one flowering plant or many, that is your personal choice. As a total novice four years ago, I quickly discovered no singular book had the answer to all my green-fingered questions, but I did yearn for one that would demystify the basics and offer me modern examples of plants and ways of gardening in my own country.

In the following pages I arm you with enough to get going and get growing. You'll still run into questions but it is my hope I have put you in good stead to at least know what questions to ask.

Use the internet, it will instantly smooth your way. Use books, information on how to grow never dates. Use social media, it'll provide you with a new community of fellow plant lovers. And use other gardeners in your area. They are more valuable than all of the above and I have never met a gardener who doesn't want to share their knowledge with a new one.

Remember Mother Nature always has the swing ball, pulling it out just when you start feeling smug. She is the director of all proceedings out there and an unpredictable one at that. Unlike painting a room or buying a new sofa, instant gratification is something you have to leave by the wayside when it comes to gardening.

Relish the process of learning something new and welcome the reconnection with the seasons.

Julia x

YOUR GUIDE TO GETTING STARTED

In this chapter I lay out the basics that allowed me to be confident in having a go. Your little garden world will become fascinating to you and noting the changes and progress along the way will help you bank knowledge, setting yourself up for an enjoyable adventure for years to come.

PLANT TYPES
PERENNIALS / ANNUALS / BIENNIALS

PLANNING YOUR PLANTING
BASIC DESIGN IDEAS / SOURCES OF INSPIRATION

GROWING
GROW FROM SEED / DIVIDE / TAKE CUTTINGS / PURCHASED PLANTS AND SEEDLINGS

CARING FOR YOUR GARDEN
EFFECTIVE WATERING / MULCHING / WEEDING / PESTS AND DISEASE / PLANT FOOD

BASIC TOOLKIT
MY ESSENTIAL GARDENING ITEMS

PLANT TYPES

—unlock your creativity—

Having a broad understanding of plant types will unlock your creativity and pathways to further knowledge. The categories below are a way to quickly filter each plant into groups that explain their growing behaviour and how they interact with the seasons. These are the key to deciding what plants you want to invest in and leave space for, and which plants are in fact not dead but simply disappear over winter!

PERENNIALS

Plants that recede down to their roots each year, to regrow, flower and seed again.

FEATURES OF PERENNIALS: They are terrific investments! If you choose to purchase established plants, you can do so with the knowledge that they will deliver year after year AND you will be able to divide and create more plants to spread around your garden as their roots become more established. Even better is being gifted a division from someone else's garden. Some will last for years and years (and may also take a few to get going, like peonies). Some may be shorter lived and start to tire after three years or so.

Tender Perennials

These are perennials that in some cold climates, won't survive their dormant period. These are often climates that are severely frost prone or under snow all winter. Best advice is to gauge the conditions where you live, and ask your gardening neighbours what they do.

Bulbs/Corms/Tubers/Rhizomes

Essentially perennial plants that grow from strange bulbous 'storage organs' of differing types.

Some of these are hardy (can handle below freezing temps) and some tender (will die if frosted). They multiply each year, so every couple of years it is worth digging them up, post flowering, to gently divide and replant your new stock elsewhere.

I'd advise looking up how to plant each type listed above as I definitely planted my peony tubers upside down and had to dig them up and replant!

Shrubs

These are perennial plants that are smaller than trees and have woody stems above the ground when dormant.

When they go dormant over winter they can either be evergreen, with leaves all year round like box hedging, camellias and rhododendrons. Or they can be deciduous, where they lose their leaves to reveal their woody stems like hydrangeas.

Shrubs are important for flower gardens as they offer structure all year round, supporting your little landscape with visual interest when your other plants have finished for the year.

ANNUALS

Plants that grow, flower, set seed and die in a single year. Often they are prolific self-seeders and will re-emerge as new plants in the same position.

FEATURES OF ANNUALS: They are celebrated for their abundant colourful blooms, especially in summer, and instant brightening and cheering up of your outside space. I've found them to be eager, fast growers when planted in their preferred positions (for example, full sun). Many will flower for months if given good care (water, deadheading) and a position they are happy with.

Many are fantastic for use in hanging planters and pots as well as adding interest to the edges of your garden.

You might spot annuals being referred to at garden centres as bedding plants.

Hardy Annuals

These are annuals that can be sown directly into the ground where you want them to grow and can tolerate cold and frosts. Often they can be sown in late autumn or early spring. Talk about low maintenance!

Half-Hardy Annuals

Plants that need some more nurturing by planting in seedling containers and in shelter away from frost before transplanting into their garden position once well established.

My garden 1st October...

...and then 6th January

BIENNIALS

Unlike annuals, biennials complete their life cycle over two years. From germination of their seed they establish their roots, stems and leaves in the first year, with the second season being their flowering, setting of seed then dying.

Once you get them in a self-seeding cycle they'll be there every year and it will seem as though they are flowering annuals with no cost!

Why is it helpful to understand these terms?
Once you understand how to identify each plant you love as existing in one of these categories, you suddenly are able to plan your garden, understanding your investment in plants and what will return each year.

This is also really helpful if you have inherited a garden. Wait a full year to see what pops up over the seasons to understand what you are working with and where plants are hiding.

Previous pages: Getting out into the garden during the year for various green-fingered jobs. **Above:** Growing perennials means your garden is often very bare going into spring, but you will be rewarded in summer and autumn. Top photo taken in early spring, bottom in early summer, with 3 months between them. In the foreground are large containers of dahlias, pansies, replacing tulips, and on the left, *Verbena bonariensis* and *Verbena rigida* ready for their seasonal show.

PLANNING YOUR PLANTING
—inspiration and tips—

"Growing a garden is like painting a picture that is never finished."

CAROLYN FERRABY – BAREWOOD

The further I got into my own garden, the more I noticed others. What people choose to grow in your area is an encouraging signal of what your environment and climate can offer your own garden. What's more, you rapidly realise that the 'decorating' of a garden is not far removed from how people nest their own homes. Plant choices and positioning can help you achieve the vibe you are after just as much as paint and furniture decisions inside.

As one of my favourite New Zealand gardeners, Carolyn Ferraby of Barewood Garden once relayed to me, 'Growing a garden is like painting a picture that is never finished.'

I think this realisation that your garden will never be done takes the pressure off. As a beginner learning about plants, it's nice to know that your garden will forgive you, constantly allowing opportunity to dig up, move, redesign and regrow.

Growing flowers comes with a lot of learning but you are rewarded by being plugged back in to Mother Nature and her seasons. I have found this to be calming, grounding and a reprieve from the intense unpredictability of the human world.

Left: The magical realm of Barewood Garden in Marlborough, with its springtime spectacle of white wisteria. **Below:** *Verbena bonariensis* is a favourite of pollinators, and I don't even mind that it's purple!

BASIC DESIGN IDEAS

Below are my key tips, taken away from attending open gardens and festivals. Even as a beginner they are a true hotspot of inspiration for those that are feeling keen. No matter the scale or style of the gardens you visit, there is always a corner/plant/idea to be pulled for your own. And if nothing at all, it is encouraging to see what passionate home gardeners have achieved in their own spaces, just with a few more years of practice.

REPETITION

This spelt bad news for my own garden which is essentially a library of every single plant I have chased down! I noticed that the gardens that I am most moved by have paid attention to repeating, grouping and reweaving plants through beds to give real substance to their aesthetic and style.

Consider choosing five plants to repeat and fill out in your own bed to get going. Just be sure to research growing heights so you know where to plant them.
LESSON: Sometimes more of less is more.

STRUCTURE VS SOFTNESS

A concept I have tiptoed around the edges of with my love of clipped topiary balls and rambling soft planting. It's a wonder that straight hard lines can be achieved with plants as much as hard landscaping, and the changing effect of this as a garden moves through the seasons. For me this is where design enters my gardening equation and opens the doors to a lot of fun! I am sure many a landscape designer fiddles with this balance but there is no reason we, as amateurs, can't either.
LESSON: Juxtaposition is where the magic lives.

LINES OF SIGHT

I've always been a fan of greeting views and buildings that channel my attention on purpose, but I can honestly say that I never really considered this as something that I could actively pursue in my own small garden. What I discovered from visiting others' gardens, is that there were some that led my eyes places or presented me with a special moment. I learned that this could be achieved in intimate spaces as much as sweeping ones.
LESSON: Atmosphere and drama can be achieved in any size garden once we consider how they might be viewed and moved through.

LAYERS AND TEXTURE

At the basic level, layers in a garden likely exist with planting shorter plants at the front and taller at the back. This is important for function and growth as much as the visual effect! What I hadn't stopped to consider is the very different vibe created by layering textures across each other, considering a moment in the garden from the ground right to the horizon. This does require some experience in that you need to know what your mature plants will look like, but forge ahead!
LESSON: Texture is just as important in a garden as it is in an interior space.

COLOUR

I've come to realise that colour in your garden behaves very differently to colour in your home. Whether or not you love all colour with wild abandon and your living room is a rainbow or a neutral, textural haven, try to approach your outside plant choices with an open mind. Your dislike of purple cushions shouldn't taint your adoption of purple blooms. Because purple in the garden is violet, indigo, lilac, plum, deep magenta and made better by being spiky, silky, airy, plump or puffy.
LESSON: Plant and petal colour adds dimension and atmosphere.

SOURCES OF INSPIRATION

The plants I have offered to you here in this book are presented in isolation. This isn't a garden planting plan, but independent options, of which some are friends, but equally could be individually poked into your own existing garden to start bringing in the good floral vibes.

If you are starting from scratch I'd suggest researching the concepts of naturalistic planting schemes which employ the clever use of mixing perennial flowering plants and grasses for a divine, modern take on a flower garden. Alternatively, the term 'cottage garden' sounds a little old-fashioned but it simply encompasses gardens that have embraced the idea of more is more with a focus on flowers over artful shrubbery, something I personally buy into pretty hard. Soft lines, undulating planting schemes, waves of seasonal flowering and an edge of chaos define this concept.

MY PERSONAL SOURCES OF INSPIRATION:

• Visit gardens local to you. Check the New Zealand Gardens Trust website to see if there are any open for wandering. Explore your local parks and gardens, notice what your neighbours have planted, even public planting on verges in town can spur an idea!

• Instagram and Pinterest are great places to gain inspiration and information. Save imagery as you go to refer back to if you need to research the names of plants you are seeing. Imagery is also really helpful to refer to when selecting plants to create a similar design, plan or vibe using the plants you can get your hands on in New Zealand.

• YouTube is a mecca for the new gardener. The answer to every question you have is on there and covered by at least five people! I find it a great way to access past series of UK-based BBC *Gardeners' World* which offers relevant practical advice (via Monty Don, the godfather of home gardening!) and glimpses of diverse home gardens around the country.

• The beauty of gardening is that the books you buy on the subject rarely date. Growing is growing and while pest control, soil management and planting combinations might change with time, basic gardening information remains super helpful! So scan the aisles of your local second-hand store for gardening reference books that you can add to your collection.

My favourite gardening books that have influenced my personal planting choices, upped my knowledge and given me a base to develop my own style are:

The Yates *Garden Guide*
Now about to move past its 79th edition, this is a must for immediate New Zealand-specific growing info, particularly helpful for identifying disease and troubleshooting.

Any books written by Monty Don
He has a lovely, lingo-free way of communicating and covers simply everything you need to know. Occasionally the advice is not as relevant to us in New Zealand, but you will fill in the gaps!

Brilliant & Wild: A Garden from Scratch in a Year **by Lucy Bellamy**
Lucy is the editor of my most loved inspiration source, the magazine *Gardens Illustrated*, and this book is simply golden for beginners. There are even some basic garden plans in the naturalistic style that could inspire you for your own. Unfortunately, there are plants she specifies that don't seem to be available here at the moment.

Wild about Weeds: Garden Design with Rebel Plants **by Jack Wallington**
The man who opened my eyes up to all plants and taught me a little respect! This is a really interesting book to help you understand many of the common plants we simply turn our back to. It's exciting to be able to give names to them.

Companion Planting in New Zealand **by Brenda Little**
A compact, easy to refer to, totally relevant guide to planting what with what. Although very focused on vegetables there is much to be learned and considered that is useful for your garden. Like chives under your dwarf apple tree!

Cut Flower Garden: Grow, Harvest & Arrange Stunning Seasonal Blooms **by Erin Benzakein of Floret Farm**
Erin is a superstar in the exploding world of flower farmers and farmer florists. Based in the chilly Washington State in the USA, she is an incredibly generous sharer that home gardeners can glean many skills from. This book has been formative in learning about great cut flowers and what I could grow for myself, as well as amazing free mini courses and downloadable information.

The Pottery Gardener: Flowers and Hens at the Emma Bridgewater Factory **by Arthur Parkinson**
A brilliant way to open your eyes up to the possibilities of flowers in containers. Offers a lot of inspiration for those with small gardens. He also talks about chooks a lot.

Dreamscapes: Inspiration and Beauty in Gardens Near and Far **by Claire Takacs**
Australian photographer Claire Takacs has become *the* world leader in capturing the essence and atmosphere of gardens around the world. This book is an armchair way to explore diverse gardens from around the world.

GROWING
—various methods—

HOW TO GROW FROM SEED

Even if you haven't grown anything since those potato heads in primary school, you are in luck as ultimately seeds *want* to grow. So with Mother Nature on your side, and a gentle reminder that it's very common for seeds not to germinate too, below is a guideline to how I get them going.

MY BEGINNER'S KIT FOR STARTING SEEDS:
Seed mix from garden centres or hardware stores. Essentially new-born plant-friendly potting mix with all the right healthy bits and nothing too strong.

Propagator – sounds serious but it's not! I have one that I use over and over as it is essentially a mini greenhouse. The little cells sit on a bio fabric that in turn sucks water through to the bases of each cell. It also has a clear plastic lid to keep things humid and cosy. It is robust and I use it year after year. I find using a propagator helps avoid overwatering my seedlings.

>   **Or use modular seed trays.** Reusing punnets from the garden centre or even egg cartons will work too! These will need to sit in a tray that you can top up with water, allowing them to suck up the moisture from the bottom of the cells. Simply use a clear plastic bag to imitate the humid conditions of the propagator during germination.

>   **Or biodegradable seed trays.** These are quite good for larger seeds that are sturdy as they emerge through the soil and after forming a few sets of leaves can be planted out into the garden complete with pot.

Larger reusable pots that you can graduate your baby seedlings to before planting out in the garden. This is commonly referred to as 'potting on'. I always save my plastic punnets I receive when buying plants from the garden centre and reuse just for this.

Gardening gloves and mask for handling dry seed mix (legionnaires' disease is real).

Trays for resting seed cells/pottles in to sap up water from their bases. I have used old roasting trays for this many a time as they are easy to top up from the edges and, if flat, allow water to be evenly delivered to the whole multi tray.

SEED SIZE
Before you begin, consider the size of your seed. Teeny seeds that look like dust are best sprinkled lightly on the surface of your seed mix-filled punnets. Spray a little water on them to help them get started, then make sure the seed trays are always kept moist by sucking in water from their bases resting in a tray of water or a propagator.

It is possible to keep them too wet too! So just monitor them daily, treat them like your babies.

Bigger seeds like sweet peas can be planted one at a time and pushed deeper into the seed mix in the punnet. Using a pencil to punch a little hole can be helpful to drop seed into and gently cover in. Erin Benzakein in her book *Cut Flower Garden* sums it up best: 'A general rule of thumb is to plant the seed twice as deep as its longest side.'

POSITIONING AND CARE

After you have filled your trays/punnets/pottles/pots with seed mix and then dressed them with their seeds, you need to offer them a very friendly environment to germinate. In the germination stage they like gentle warmth and moisture to get their first shoots to pop through the soil. A sheltered bright spot like a back porch, windowsill or even kitchen table can work.

Humidity is helpful too, achieved by the clear lid of your propagator or even a loosely draped plastic bag. Once it gets warmer and your seedlings are growing, leave off the lid or cover during the day, returning them to cosy in the evenings.

Propagators have a water delivery system that is easily topped up and delivers an ideal amount of water to your seedling cells. Alternatively, if using seedling punnets, they need to have their bases seated in a tray topped up with water so they can hydrate from their bases, avoiding the risk of washing seeds away by watering from the top. Daily checks are needed so your punnets don't dry out. Equally, you want to avoid having them sitting in water full-time as this will deliver nasty problems like mildew and seedling death/non-germination. It's a juggle that just requires regular checks.

Once my seedlings get a couple of sets of leaves, I then leave any covers off and they naturally harden off with the fluctuations in heat during the day in their covered outdoor position. Keeping them covered for too long will make them spindly as they grow in their luxurious warm home.

POTTING ON AND GRADUATING TO THE GARDEN

Graduating my seedlings by grouping into larger pots is something that I do to make room in my propagator to grow more. This is called 'potting on' and I generally fill their new home with seed mix as opposed to other options.

In terms of moving the new plants to the garden, initially I took inspiration from the size of the smaller seedlings available in trays that I would buy at the garden centre. Once mine appeared a similar size and seemed healthy off they would go! This usually looks to be about 3–4 sets of leaves.

Once in the wild of your garden, your little plants will have a target on their back for birds looking to have an aggressive scratch around in the newly disturbed soil around them.

I combat this by building a wee stick fortress around the most exposed ones to protect them.

Be sure to research the ideal growing conditions for your plant that you have brought to life. Don't waste your effort of all this early care to then plant in a shady position in the garden when it requires full sun to be the best plant it can be. Don't worry if you have some failures, it is guaranteed in gardening!

SOWING DIRECT INTO THE GARDEN

Can your seeds be planted direct in the ground where you would like them to grow? Read your seed packet, note from seller or look up online. Some plants hate to be moved from pot to ground, so it's important to understand the needs of what you are planting.

If so, just wait until the ground warms up a bit in mid to late spring. Look for the arrival of annual weeds starting to green up the bare parts of your garden – this is a good sign that the ground is warm enough and ready.

You can sow seeds any time through to late spring/early summer, after that I'd suggest purchasing already established seedlings to plug into the garden to give you a chance for some colour before the frosts. Also be sure to mark the location of your seed so you know not to weed it out.

HOW TO DIVIDE

Dividing often requires some muscle and never quite looks like it does in the books, but it is a remarkably easy way to increase the population of your favourite plants in the garden. Cheap too.

Division of your perennials is best in autumn or spring. Dig up your plant using a spade or garden fork if available. Give the plant a bit of a shake to remove clumps of dirt and give you a clear view of its shape. Use a hose to remove soil if you like.

On occasion you can prize the roots apart and make divisions simply using your hands. If not, use a sharp spade to slice through the clump.

You may continue to divide a few times, however err on the side of caution to ensure you have good healthy root stock in each section.

Replant your divisions, water and hope for the best!

HOW TO TAKE CUTTINGS

Cuttings can be taken from perennials and shrubs as a way of propagating new plants. Taking advantage of fresh, strong, early spring growth is best. A basic beginner approach is to select a healthy, non-flowering stem from a plant, cleanly cutting off a tip with at least two sets of leaves, making the cut just below a node. This is where the plant will generate its new roots from! Your cutting should be around 10–15 cm.

You can then either dip the end of the stem into a rooting hormone to give your cutting the best chance (found easily at garden centres) or skip ahead and simply plant it in a small pot with seed raising mix or similar that is free draining. Plant your cutting in the mix, up to below the first leaf and water well.

Place in a well-lit sheltered spot but out of direct sunlight and watch for the arrival of fresh green growth.

HOW TO PLANT OUT PURCHASED PLANTS

This is an easy way to start adding to your garden as a new gardener, and can be surprisingly affordable particularly if purchasing perennials for a smaller garden.

Using a trowel or niwashi tool, prepare a hole that your seedling or plant will comfortably fit into, loosening up the dirt around the base and sides to welcome new roots. It is important that the plant sits at the same level as it did in the punnet or pot. I often sprinkle in a handful of quality potting mix if planting into average soil.

Gently fill in around your seedling or plant with your soil, firming the soil around it with care so as not to damage the roots. Always finish off with a good soak of water to allow the new soil to sink in closely around it, leaving no air pockets.

Below: Using my trusty niwashi tool to plant snapdragon seedlings in early summer. **Right:** Planting out perennials purchased on sale from the garden centre in autumn.

CARING FOR YOUR GARDEN
—basic knowledge—

HOW TO EFFECTIVELY WATER YOUR GARDEN

Firstly, dial into your garden, even if it is a small town of pots or garden beds. Notice the plump strength of your plants after a good rain, they practically glow with wellbeing (rainwater actually contains nitrate, necessary for the development of lush foliage). Then have a wander after a scorcher and see the distinct wilt and flop to their leaves. This is what a thirsty plant looks like vs a hydrated one, an obvious message that water is required. Another immediate test is to sink your finger into the soil to the second knuckle. If you feel moisture beyond the top layer, all is well for now. If dry at your fingertips, it's time to top up.

Now the BIG clincher. When should you deliver this water, and how? By all accounts first thing in the morning is the best, giving important hydration to the plants to cope with heat but time enough for their leaves to be dry before they go to bed. Soggy foliage in the cool of the evening can encourage disease like mildew. However, for gardening to be enjoyable it also needs to fit into your own schedule, so an easy rule of thumb is to water after 6 pm and before 10 am. Watering during the heat of the day, under direct sunlight risks wastage through

Deeply watering your beds and letting them dry between times will encourage your plants to develop deeper root systems, vital to their resilience of dry spells and challenging water restrictions that might come.

evaporation, and droplets of water on leaves can also magnify sunlight and scorch your plant.

While it feels like the right thing to do, quick daily top-ups of water does more harm than good in the long run. Pots and newly planted out seedlings are the exception here, with their greater potential for evaporation and baby root systems so close to the surface. Daily watering in the height of summer is sometimes needed for them, or at least every second day. In contrast, for garden beds, aim for deep soaks 1–3 times a week depending on the heat and natural rainfall you get. This is where garden watering systems come into their own, as you want to water a bed of plants for 45–60 minutes at a time. Essentially, less frequency of watering but for longer periods.

Deeply watering your beds and letting them dry between times will encourage your plants to develop deeper root systems, vital to their resilience of dry spells and challenging water restrictions that might come.

While water restrictions will often dictate how you are able to deliver your water, with bans on hoses and sprinklers at different levels, installing and reviewing your systems is a good idea.

Garden specific irrigation systems are very easy to come by and install, with starter kits available at all hardware stores. Trust me when I say, if you don't have one in your garden, certainly go chat to one of those helpful employees in the garden aisle and see what you can come up with within your budget. Having a system makes watering a breeze. You can also pick up timers which will allow you to plan your

watering, even if you are away. There are many options that include above-ground sprayers or in-ground drippers. If you already have above-ground, do a quick review with them turned on, making sure all are directed properly into your garden beds, not wasting your precious water by soaking the driveway instead. In-ground drippers are a fantastic option as they drastically reduce the amount of water that evaporates into thin air and there are many plants that frown at having their blooms and foliage hosed down constantly.

If you are a hand waterer, using your hose, make sure you have a good spray head on it that allows you to easily control how much water you are using and where you are directing it. When watering pots, my usual routine is to water each until I see water coming out the bottom. This may be much longer than you previously thought. When hand watering the garden, you are looking to soak about the top 30 cm of soil in your beds. To help you understand how much time this might take, use a bamboo chopstick to plunge into the sprayed soil. If wet soil has stuck to it, this is a good sign the water is heading down towards the roots.

This can feel surprisingly time-consuming if you have previously flashed your sprayer around to just visually dampen the surface, but it is important for the resilience of your garden to get a good soaking. And walking around your garden with a hose or watering can is a relaxing activity in itself.

As our earth is warming up and water becomes a more precious resource, consider ways to harvest rainwater using storage tanks and tapping into your home's gutters.

MULCHING

To top off your calculated watering, you want to give your soil the best chance of retaining it. This is when mulching comes into play. Organic options like pea straw, chopped up leaves, grass clippings and bark work well, but also are best for specific plantings, so do a little research first. These have a double-edged benefit of decomposing and adding nutrients to your bed over time. Your aim with any of them is to create a barrier between your living earth and the brutality of the sun, reducing evaporation, levelling out soil temperature and limiting the washing away of nutrients.

WEEDING

Weeds are simply plants growing where you personally don't want them. I actually grow many rebel plants in my garden on purpose as I like their flowers and they do well in difficult spots! But I certainly edit them back and keep an eye on their super spreading tendencies.

Keeping on top of weeding means your plants have less competition for water and nutrients. Usually I have a big effort in late winter when my garden (and gardening mind)

are coming back to life. I trawl the garden in sections with my kneeling pad and niwashi tool, doing my best to get all the imposters out from the root. It feels tough but is very satisfying. As a grower of perennials I find that as they leaf up in my garden, they vastly reduce the space for weeds to take hold. Mulching also suppresses them, removing their much-needed sunlight.

PESTS AND DISEASE

Certain pests tend to thrive in certain climates, so I would always use a local gardener as your first port of call with a specific issue. It is true that individual plants are prone to specific attacks of insects and disease, all treated differently to top it off! I would recommend you research symptoms online to try to identify your issue then look for solutions that suit you.

These days there are bountiful, environmentally friendly sprays to use as both a preventative and treatment, something that will become a personal choice for you. The aisle of your hardware store or garden centre is rich in solutions and I'd recommend consulting with a shop assistant to help guide your choice. There is also a universe of home-made remedies available for you to search online and experiment with.

Previous page: Your watering rotation will be transformed by using a multi-setting nozzle on your hose. Water containers until you see water emerging from the bottom. **Above:** Springtime weeding kit. **Right:** I collected autumn leaves which we then quickly shredded by sucking through the leaf blower before spreading across my garden beds as a protective winter mulch. Where possible, shred your leaves. Using a lawnmower is an option.

If you notice a plant is looking wilted with no other apparent symptoms like spotted, mildewy, rusty or curling leaves, always check the underside of its leaves closely. So many times it is here that I have found the tiniest mites sucking the life blood out of my plants.

I'll admit that I am less preventative than I am treatment based as mostly I seem to get by with very little spraying needed. This tends to change between seasons and weather conditions.

PLANT FOOD

I have largely found that caring the best I can for my soil and being diligent with watering has meant that I very rarely fertilise my plants during their season. Of course this is entirely due to the make-up of the soil I started with and its relatively fertile, free-draining ways.

Like pest control there are a million options out there for you to explore in aid of fertilising your garden beds. Mulching with natural, decomposing product is a great way to begin feeding and improving your soil over time. Once a year I also gently fork in blood and bone, sheep/chicken pellets and rich compost to my vege/cutting garden and poorer soil areas during winter when my plants are in bed or the soil is empty.

There is no limit to the reading that you could do on soil improvement including no-dig and permaculture principles. Home composting is a fascinating and sometimes challenging adventure that you will no doubt explore as the garden bug grows in you. But for the meantime, know that adding rich organic matter to your soil is doing good.

Additionally, you can help your growers along during their season by applying fertiliser in dry or liquid form. It's my containers that I concentrate on most here. Some earth-friendly options involving seaweed, blood and bone and minerals are readily available to you. Not to mention the scrolling benefits of your weekly food waste to amplify your plants.

My advice to you is to chat to a gardener, gardening aisle/garden centre staff or search the internet to seek the best options for both you, your soil and the types of plants you are growing.

BASIC TOOLKIT
—for the beginner gardener—

1. Garden twine
It's so handy to have a roll of string at the ready. You'll use it for supporting floppy sweet peas on a trellis or gently tying tall stemmed plants to stakes for support.

2. Quality secateurs
Avoid the frustration of cheap ones and buy the best you can with your budget. You will use them for cutting back your perennials in winter and general pruning of roses and shrubs.

3. Slim-nosed garden snips
Mostly I harvest all my flowers with these daintier secateurs. It is easier to be precise with cuts to enable your plant to continue flowering. Also use for general deadheading and conditioning flower stems for the vase.

4. Iron stakes
I have used straight bamboo for vertical staking in the past, but attractive iron ones look terrific and last for life!

5. Bamboo hoops
Really versatile supports you will use garden wide during the flowering season. Buy in packs from the hardware store.

6. Kneeling pad
While not vital, I find this wee pad makes largescale weeding efforts a little easier to deal with!

7. Watering can
For when you need to water in your planted out seedlings and general watering when summer restrictions kick in.

8. Tough, reusable garden bag
Vital for your winter perennial clean up and any pruning you do. I have multiple bags that I fill before taking to the green waste depot.

9. Spade and fork
Do your best to buy quality here so you don't have handles flying off! Mine are mostly used for digging up and dividing perennials in autumn and spring.

10. Mask
I wear one without fail everytime I open a bag of potting mix, compost or mulch to protect from the dangerous airborne bacteria that can cause legionnaires' disease.

11. Gardening gloves
Any will do and you will wear them out! But they'll save your hands from constant grub, add protection when handling potting mix and make largescale tidying up much easier.

12. Non-kinking hose and control nozzle
Any hose will of course do! But stepping up the quality will reduce kinking frustrations while on your watering rounds. It's also important to have a hose attachment with flow options so you can control your water application and avoid wasting water.

13. Hand trowel
Easier than a spade for small-scale hole digging.

14. Niwashi tool
My most versatile and handy garden tool. Brilliant for spiking weeds out from the roots and planting out seedlings in the garden.

Next page: The garden is revived after a spring shower.

{ 0 1 / 1 2 }

Sweet peas

Of anything I will ever grow, sweet peas will have a special, delicious spot in my gardening lifeline. It was these friendly, uncomplicated creatures that became my 'first' flowers. First flowers to greet me driving in my gate, first flowers to pose for me in the soft morning light, first blooms I could cut for my home and experience the joy of taking frothy bunches to give to others. If there was a kickstart for growing flowers, you've found it here.

Left: A lush bunch of 'Blue Shift' sweet peas in a second-hand vase.

SWEET PEAS

LATIN NAME	*Lathyrus odoratus*
PLACE OF ORIGIN	Sicily, southern Italy and Aegean Islands.
PLANT TYPE	Annual vine with delicate, butterfly-like blooms growing on supported frame 1–2 metres. Dwarf varieties growing 20–60 cm high available.
FLOWERING	Late spring through summer only if well-watered and deadheaded.
GROWING CONDITIONS	Full sun, well-watered and well-fed soil.
WHEN TO PLANT	Sow direct in autumn or spring. Alternatively raise undercover to plant out in late spring after risk of frost. Transfer purchased punnets of seedlings in spring.
SPACING	20 cm
WHERE TO PLANT	Tall climbing vines running up trellis, fence, freestanding teepee or other supports.
SUITABLE FOR CONTAINERS	Yes
PINCHING	Yes but not essential. Pinching at four sets of leaves will create bushier plants.
CUT AND COME AGAIN	Yes
STAKING	Ideally needs support to climb otherwise will ramble through garden.
SUSCEPTIBLE TO	Powdery mildew and quick dying off when too dry.
TOXICITY	Yes, seeds are mildly poisonous to humans.

—How to grow—
SWEET PEAS

Sweet peas are bushy climbers with surprisingly brittle, twisted vines and broad, soft green leaves and tendrils. On slim straight stems they produce delicate, butterfly-esque blooms that can be luxuriously fragrant and coloured.

I often allow my wall of sweet peas to self-seed, resulting in the eager growth of foliage over winter and very early flowering in spring. It's possible to sow them yourself, direct in place in late autumn for an early spring flowering, as well as in spring for a summer display. Alternatively you can raise seeds undercover to plant out in spring or buy strong seedlings in punnets to plant out.

Ultimately, sweet peas are eager, satisfying growers if they have full sun, a structure to climb and plenty of food and water. Seaweed fertilisers, sheep pellets/manure will all please them. Consider them growing teenagers!

Ideas for structures are endless. You could use a trellis, sections of steel foundation mesh leaning or stapled to the fence, teepees made from bamboo, spindly branches plunged into the soil or even a tree! They are a vine so thrive being able to ramble over something.

Sweet peas definitely start to struggle in the intense heat of high summer so diligent monitoring and watering is a must if you want to keep them around for as long as possible. You can increase their life span (as well as your haul of flowers for the vase) with regular deadheading. For best results, once or twice a week snip off every single bloom, including any partially open buds. This signals to the plant that it needs to work hard to create more buds to reach its end goal of forming seeds.

Continue to snip off any developing seed pods until you can tell the plant is starting to look a little bedraggled, then allow your seeds to dry on the plant, until the pods are the colour of brown cardboard. You can harvest these to save and grow next year, give to a friend, or you can allow the pods to spring open themselves to self-seed a new crop in the same position.

Watering is very important for sweet peas. They are 'head in the sun with moist feet' kind of plants. They suffer almost instantly when too dry, and stress to the plant allows powdery mildew to sneak in. Dense planting and the resulting lack of air circulation on dewy nights acts as great conditions for the fungus. It appears as a white powdery residue across the leaves and it can be treated early with a number of home-made remedies that vary from mouthwash mixes, baking soda, dish soap and even milk! The internet will provide an abundance of options for you to experiment with. In my experience powdery mildew wins in the end and will eventually take down the plant at the end of its season.

Once you are satisfied with the amount of seeds you have collected, it's likely your plant is looking pretty scraggly. To clean up your bed simply rip out from the roots.

Right: 'Blue Shift' changing from deep magenta to blue as flowers mature. Photos taken over six days.

MY FAVOURITES

Look out for seeds or seedlings by Dr Keith Hammett, a world-renowned sweet pea breeder based here in New Zealand. My favourites are 'High Scent' for its fragrance and long stems and 'Blue Shift' for its fascinating movement from deep magenta to blue as the flowers mature. 'Almost Black' looks fabulous contrasted against the soft, muted green of the foliage.

Left and above: To keep your vines producing flowers it's important to harvest every single bloom from the plants at least once a week. **Right:** 'Blue Shift' going mad with home-grown bearded irises, aquilegia, renga renga flowers and elder foliage.

IN THE GARDEN

Sweet peas offer a delicate ramble within a garden landscape. A lovely plant to soften the straight lines of fencing, clipped shrubs and hard landscaping. Due to being such eager growers, they are a fantastic option to experiment with growing flowers for the first time, and are addictive at that!

Mostly I grow mine in a skinny garden bed against a warm sunny fence in my driveway. The effect is a frilly, colourful wall of interest at almost no expense. I have experimented with growing them unsupported within my perennials, and they found the strong body of my fennel plants a great structure to zigzag up, their little blooms hovering, as if from nowhere, around the tops of the other plants.

The biggest struggle I have with these plants is leaving them in the ground for their seeds to develop long after they look scraggly and tired. Many may choose to rip them out before this, knowing they might purchase seeds or seedlings the following year, thus dodging the burnt ugly look of their maturity.

Left: My sweet pea crop is all self-seeded resulting in very early flowering in spring. **Above:** Sweet peas and developing seed pods in the morning light.

Left: A large haul of rambling 'High Scent' chopped for the vase. Only when I have a lot of plants do I choose to take so much of the main stalks. **Right:** Sweet peas with white bluebells, aquilegia foliage, forget-me-nots, apple blossom and a single tulip. **Next page:** My 'Almost Black' sweet peas mixed in with friends in full swing! Each year I play with growing different varieties, some from seed and some picked up cheaply in seedling punnets from the garden centre.

FOR THE VASE

Sweet peas are fabulous cut flowers, bringing their delicate, winding limbs and sweet scent into the home. I would describe them as having a moderate vase life of 4–5 days with their best potential found in just-opened blooms.

After cutting get them into deep water straight away before preparing them for your vase. Gently trim off all foliage below the water line of your vessel and give a quick fresh snip of the stem before positioning.

If I have lots of sweet peas I will get aggressive and cut long limbs of foliage and flowers as this looks wild and beautiful in a vase alone or mingled with friends. Of course this does limit future bounty from the plant but it's a worthy sacrifice.

Sweet peas look sweet and delicate collected en masse in a small vase, or if you are lucky to have long stems earlier in the season, mixed with other seasonal flowers gives a lightness to any bunch.

Fennel

As bizarre as this might sound, fennel is one of my all-time favourite plants to grow for both my garden and vase. As a beginner it is helpful to employ things that really want to grow, and fennel does just that with enthusiasm. Its main attraction was its beautiful, structural umbellifer-type flower in that acid greeny-yellow, but I have grown to appreciate its ferny foliage and reliable return appearance just as much.

Left: Fennel flowers with home-grown bearded iris, mini chrysanthemums, kōwhai flowers, geums, aquilegia flowers and foliage combined with a peony grown by my cousins on their peony farm.

COMMON NAME

FENNEL

LATIN NAME	*Foeniculum vulgare*
PLACE OF ORIGIN	Mediterranean
PLANT TYPE	Perennial often grown as an annual reaching 2 m tall and creating clumps. Self-seeds readily.
FLOWERING	Mid/late spring through to late autumn.
GROWING CONDITIONS	Full sun and fertile, well-drained soil.
WHEN TO PLANT	Raise seeds undercover to plant out or sow direct in position in spring after the frosts. Alternatively purchase as seedlings to easily transplant into garden.
SPACING	50 cm +. Matures to very tall and bushy.
WHERE TO PLANT	Back of your garden bed, ideally with space to spread bushy limbs out.
SUITABLE FOR CONTAINERS	Yes
PINCHING	No
CUT AND COME AGAIN	Yes
STAKING	Yes, but mostly to keep it off neighbouring plants.
SUSCEPTIBLE TO	Aphids
TOXICITY	No

—How to grow—

FENNEL

Fennel really wants to grow so this is a very reassuring plant to have as a beginner. In this instance, I am referring to growing the herb fennel as opposed to Florence fennel which is grown to harvest its tasty bulb. Herb fennel still offers lots of extras that many other flowering perennials don't, with great leaves for cooking plus enormous amounts of seeds for your pantry.

Raise from seed in trays undercover and plant out after frosts are finished in spring, or direct sow in place from mid-spring. You can also pick up an inexpensive punnet of them at the hardware store or vege table at the garden centre.

It took me a while to catch on but in my climate fennel behaves as a perennial, not an annual as I first assumed. I used to rip out the entire plant once it looked worn out in winter, and while I still do sometimes due to prolific self-seeding, mostly I just hack back my now established clumps. Continue to harvest flowers for your vase to encourage the plant to keep producing them. Letting flowers form seeds later in the season makes for an easy, fantastic harvest for your pantry and also provides winter nibbles for birds. In winter I then prune back all foliage to around 20 cm and watch as the foliage regenerates and the plants prepare for spring again. Established plants seem to leaf up and grow considerably in height before they start offering flowers in late spring to summer. They look like big green fluffy masses before starting to offer their starbursts.

Keep your eyes peeled as fennel is a prolific self-seeder and you will spot ferny, new seedlings emerging in the surrounding garden in spring.

Previous page: Roadside buttercups and long limbs of fennel standing guard in my kitchen. **Right:** My fennel patch in late spring. I regularly harvest the flowers and foliage but will leave much to dry on the plant for birds and harvesting in the autumn. I cut this stand right down to allow new growth in winter.

Above: Fennel and marigolds getting tonal in the vege garden. **Opposite page:** The dried heads of fennel, heavy with seeds for birds and use in cooking; fennel in the garden supporting a rambling sweet pea.

IN THE GARDEN

Without enough room, fennel can be somewhat bolshy in the garden. All elbows and throwing shade on the littlies surrounding it, but the flipside is it can also offer great support and protection for flimsier friends nearby. It wants to grow so much that I simply hack back parts of it at the base to reduce its impact and thin it out a little.

Its consistently reliable, healthy growth is very appealing when trying to imagine what a bed might look like each season. I have even used it to support sweet peas, winding and twisting up towards the sun. This had a very romantic, rambling effect.

For a different vibe explore planting Bronze fennel *Foeniculum vulgare* 'Rubrum' or *Foeniculum vulgare* 'Bronze'.

FOR THE VASE

It's hard for me to rank my most favourite feature of fennel as a cut flower. The umbellifer shape of its flowers is so wonderfully abstract when mixed with others, while the chartreuse of its tiny petals seems so weirdly bright at times. And it lasts so long in a vase I often rescue it from a spent arrangement, re-snip the stem and place in a new one.

Due to its generous growth and height, you can get gutsy with your arrangements, harvesting full length limbs of flowers and foliage to display in a tall, weighty vase. Kind of like importing a whole garden into the house. More is more!

When cutting, snip above a branching stem to encourage new growth. Immature fennel flowers picked too early can flop in the vase with their softer stems, so always choose when their pollen is bright and the resulting stems are strong.

Left: Home-grown fennel with aquilegia, geums, purple toadflax and lush gifted peonies. **Above:** A quirky bedside collection of fennel, cosmos and leek flower.

{03/12}

Verbena bonariensis

Every year it gets harder to pick a favourite, but *Verbena bonariensis* (or VB as I call it) brings all the wild, generous and romantic vibes I pursue for my patch. It is my number one. It looks good with everybody. It flowers longer than anyone else. It is bee, butterfly, then bird heaven. It self-seeds like a maniac but I just merrily pot up all the babies to give away so that others catch the VB love too. I can honestly declare I'll never have a garden without it.

Left: A late spring riot of tonal mauves and purple featuring *Verbena bonariensis*, *Verbena rigida*, purple toadflax, sweet peas, foxgloves, honeysuckle, a spray of white 'Iceberg' roses and a single 'Blue Moon' rose.

COMMON NAME

PURPLETOP VERVAIN, ARGENTINIAN VERVAIN, VERBENA
(or let's call it VB!)

LATIN NAME	*Verbena bonariensis* (we will also cover *Verbena rigida*)
PLACE OF ORIGIN	South America
PLANT TYPE	Tall airy perennial with long cylindrical stems, sparse leaves and tightly clustered violet flowers. Will grow to 1.8 m.
FLOWERING	Late spring to late autumn.
GROWING CONDITIONS	Full sun
WHEN TO PLANT	Raise seeds undercover to plant out or sow direct in position in mid-late spring. Seeds are slow to germinate. Transplant purchased plants at any time, spring to early autumn.
SPACING	30–60 cm
WHERE TO PLANT	Due to its height it is excellent for the back of a bed, but its airy nature means that it will weave between other plants in the middle without being disruptive.
SUITABLE FOR CONTAINERS	Yes
PINCHING	No
CUT AND COME AGAIN	Yes
STAKING	Yes
SUSCEPTIBLE TO	Occasional powdery mildew.
TOXICITY	No

—How to grow—
VERBENA BONARIENSIS

Welcome to the plant you didn't imagine could make your garden look so cool! VB is very easy to get going from seed and hasn't been readily available in garden centres in New Zealand until recently. Try smaller, speciality nurseries, seed providers or online trading platforms where you can get seed straight from gardeners themselves.

Raise undercover in seed trays and do not be dismayed if your VB seeds are the last ones to germinate. Plant out in late spring or early summer and protect from birds as they get established. I build mini fences around my seedlings using sticks which works most of the time. Bear in mind that the mature plants are vigorous and will take up around 50 cm of space – they will reach well over a metre tall even in their first season.

VB only tolerates very little shade, so pick a good bright spot. Its intense efforts to grow will mean that while it will make it in a shady spot, it will be particularly spindly and heading off in crazy directions searching for sun.

Once you have VB, it tends to stick around, self-seeding throughout the garden much further than you might expect. Over the flowering season you will observe how new tiny flowers push through the head of the bloom, while seeds develop below. So it is flowering and seeding all at once! You quickly learn to identify its tiny red-stemmed seedlings meaning you can easily stay on top of it and patrol your garden borders. Particularly important if you live in the countryside. If you want to make use of these new self-seeded plants, leave them in place until they have a couple of sets of leaves before re-potting up or moving.

Verbena bonariensis is considered a three-year perennial, meaning that beyond its third season flowering it will start to under-perform. I leave my plant, complete with seed heads to be feasted on by birds during the early winter months before cutting all stems back down to around 20 cm from the ground. In an early winter garden, even the seed heads on tall stalks give structure. You will notice it starts to create a woody base, typical of a mature plant. Due to its prolific self-seeding, it doesn't feel scary to pull out your tired mature plants knowing that you won't be missing out the following season.

Previous page: *Verbena bonariensis* and its interesting blooms that produce new flowers while forming seed below them as the season goes on.
Right: The sweeping heights reached by *Verbena bonariensis* even in its first season, providing it has good sun.

MY FAVOURITES

Through some extremely bizarre occurrence, I ended up with a slightly different species, *Verbena rigida* springing up in my garden. And I am so pleased! While still with that airy, open form, *Verbena rigida* grows only to around 60 cm and has a slightly more conical appearance to its little purple flowers. This species is excellent for the front or middle of a bed, weaving through its neighbouring plants.

I have noticed it also behaves differently by sending out runners for its new plants in the spring. I still chop back to around 20 cm in winter, but notice that there is less growth on those older stems as opposed to its new plants surrounding it. And it doesn't seem to self-seed quite as prolifically.

Left: Tall arms of *Verbena bonariensis* in beside its shorter growing cousin, *Verbena rigida*.
Right: *Verbena bonariensis* and *Verbena rigida* growing well in a large pot, pictured in late spring.
Below: It's important to learn to identify the tiny, red-stemmed seedlings of VB to prevent it from escaping your property. **Bottom:** *Verbena rigida* with its slightly elongated flowering tips.

IN THE GARDEN

Firstly, don't be fooled when people nod in understanding when you mention you have *Verbena bonariensis*. Most will be thinking of the far more common 'verbena' which is often treated as an annual and a front of border ground cover.

VB brings you whimsy, structure and drama. My stand of it has always been a magnet to visitors as they marvel at its odd and very tall square-sided stems, topped with purple puff flowers.

I have loved planting it en masse as well as placing it within garden beds where it squirms up through its neighbours.

I also grow a stand of VB and *Verbena rigida* in a large pot. I have learned my lessons here, knowing that it will fry in a second if not regularly watered in the heat. That is why my pot is now right next to the tap!

I grow my own plants of both species mixed in with echinacea, rudbeckia, lupins, fennel and friends. To me they are deliciously rambling and architectural at the same time.

FOR THE VASE

Grow more than one plant in your garden as you'll definitely want to cut huge long stems of it. So plan ahead so you don't pillage your garden scape for your interior one!

VB has an incredible vase life. I love to have super tall limbs of it on a mantel or equivalent against the wall. The sheer length and graphic shape of it brings terrific drama and a scale that is really hard to achieve with many other plants. It is equally appealing in mixed arrangements and it is not uncommon for me to pluck stems out of one vase, give a quick trim and put in another while its vase mates head for the compost heap.

When harvesting for an arrangement, have a think about where you will cut a length from. I try to pick from the back of the plant where a missing central stem won't be too obvious. Snip just above a set of side shoots and you will notice new growth forming in that intersection.

Left and above: *Verbena bonariensis* provides an exciting opportunity to display arrangements with scopey height. It has a terrific vase life. Pictured artwork by Fleur Wickes.
Next page: A gaggle of seasonal summer blooms hydrating, ready to be arranged.

{04/12}

Nemesia

My love for the tall and whimsical has been an unfortunate barrier to finding low, garden edge plants that I love. But the barrier was broken by nemesia and I have eagerly encouraged its self-seeding through my garden, prising up seedlings to fill yet another gap with its pretty little blooms.

Left: Sweet bubbles of nemesia with nasturtium foliage, pansies, purple toadflax and aquilegia.

NEMESIA

LATIN NAME	*Nemesia caerulea*
PLACE OF ORIGIN	South Africa
PLANT TYPE	Annual or half-hardy perennial in cooler climates. Small pointed leaves and multi-lobed petals growing 20–40 cm high with a spreading nature.
FLOWERING	Spring through autumn.
GROWING CONDITIONS	Full sun and part shade, moist but well-drained soil. In hotter climates, aim for part shade.
WHEN TO PLANT	Raise seeds undercover to plant out or sow direct in position in late spring. Alternatively purchase potted up plants to transfer into your garden.
SPACING	15 cm
WHERE TO PLANT	Front of garden bed or in pots and hanging baskets.
SUITABLE FOR CONTAINERS	Yes
PINCHING	Yes but not essential. Pinching at around 5 cm will create bushier plants.
CUT AND COME AGAIN	Yes
STAKING	No
SUSCEPTIBLE TO	Dying off in the heat and powdery mildew.
TOXICITY	No

Above: The nemesia in my garden has been free to self-seed and in turn has morphed in colour through purple to pastels and pink.

—How to grow—
NEMESIA

In my climate (Canterbury, New Zealand) nemesia is not only an endlessly flowering perennial, it is a very pleasing self-seeder. In warmer areas it may behave as an annual, dying after it has finished flowering or perhaps succumbing to heat. Just make sure you keep them happy with lots of water and, if possible, some shade during the day.

Nemesia is a case of giving it a go. Jump online and have an explore of the various fun options available to you or keep an eye out at the garden centre for easy opportunities to plop directly into your garden.

If growing from seed, start undercover and move mature seedlings into the garden after the frosts in late spring. Alternatively, indicated by its keen self-seeding, plant directly in place in autumn in warmer climates and spring for cooler.

Once nemesia is in your garden it requires no special care. If you notice most of its flowers beginning to form seed heads, gently cut back all the upper growth to make way for a new round. It will look a little ragged for a few weeks, but new growth and flowers will quickly follow. Don't be surprised if your nemesia flowers all year round. In warmer climates it might perform best in the cooler months, buttoning off over the heat of summer.

Right: Low-lying white nemesia brightens up the edges of my garden.

MY FAVOURITES

While eventual self-seeding may morph your nemesia back to pinks
and purples, there are so many fun ones to get going, either by
seed or buying interesting varieties at the garden centre. In my own
garden I have 'Misty White' as a simple little white plant amid a sea
of green. I think I started out with mauve 'Pixie Storm' which has
found all shades of pink and purple in its self-seeding. I have my eye
on 'Bordeaux', a deep crimson with yellow centres and 'Raspberries
and Cream', which is exactly how it sounds! There are fabulous
bicolour seed packs to be snapped up too, just keep your eyes open
or go for a search locally online.

NEMESIA

Nemesia is a lovely plant to pop in around the base of my potted up trees. This adds a cheerful interest, bubbling up over the edges.

Left: White nemesia with clover, forget-me-nots, Mexican daisy, cornflowers and a single fading anemone.

73

Left and below: Nemesia peeping over the edge of a wine barrel where it is underplanted around a dwarf apple tree. It's easy to forget low-lying plants but they provide much needed interest, particularly around a garden's edges. **Right:** Nemesia with thalictrum foliage and twisty thyme flowers. **Next page:** An early autumn haul of rudbeckia, sedum, dahlias, penstemon, hollyhocks, bog sage, clematis, lupins, snapdragons, Japanese anemones and strawberries.

IN THE GARDEN

This is my 'always there' plant. A nemesia flower can be found in my garden all year round with surges of growth in spring and autumn. The best feature of it, for me, is its self-seeding all over the show. This doesn't feel invasive at all, as any seedlings out of place are very easily and quickly pricked out and moved to a new position or potted up to give away.

The very interesting result of this self-seeder is that each wee plant has morphed into a different pink or purple tone, straying away from the mauve of the original plant. This gives a subtle ombre effect around the edges of the garden and in pots beside the back door. The white clumps I have in predominately part shade don't seem to self-seed, but slowly expand with each year.

It's a lovely plant to pop in around the base of my potted up trees, adding a cheerful interest, bubbling up over the edges.

FOR THE VASE

On first looks, this doesn't really put its hand up as a
great cut flower due to its low-growing habit and leaf-clad
stems. But it is a fantastic filler in a mixed bunch, adding
low support to keep everything upright.

To prepare, I find it easiest to strip all lower leaves off
each stem as you pick them. There will be more leaves
than flowers that you have picked, but a quick run of two
fingers down the stem will get rid of them efficiently.

{ 0 5 / 1 2 }

Knautia macedonica

Knautia (a silent 'k'), with its small crimson fuzzball flowers atop long slim stalks, has got to be one of the best 'supporting' acts in my garden. She's not the show pony, she's the groom, keeping everyone around her united and gently filling in the gaps.

Left: The vivid crimson tops of sweet *Knautia macedonica*, nemesia, heuchera, astilbe flowers and foliage and *Scabiosa* 'Fama White'.

KNAUTIA or SCABIOUS

LATIN NAME	*Knautia macedonica*
PLACE OF ORIGIN	Balkans
PLANT TYPE	Perennial growing to 80 cm, creating clumps and gently self-seeding.
FLOWERING	Late spring through to autumn.
GROWING CONDITIONS	Full sun with well-drained soil.
WHEN TO PLANT	Sow direct in position in autumn, lightly covered with soil. Raise seedlings undercover in early spring to plant out in early summer. Alternatively purchase potted plants to transplant into the garden from spring to autumn. Mature plants can be divided easily to be moved in spring. Cuttings can also be made over warm months. Get good root growth started in a cup of water then transfer into small pots with potting mix before transplanting into position when healthy green growth is showing.
SPACING	50 cm +. Can be planted more sparingly as will mature in size and self-seed over time.
WHERE TO PLANT	Perfect for the middle of a garden bed.
SUITABLE FOR CONTAINERS	Yes
PINCHING	No
CUT AND COME AGAIN	Yes
STAKING	No
SUSCEPTIBLE TO	Mostly disease free.
TOXICITY	No

—How to grow—
KNAUTIA MACEDONICA

The addition of knautia to my garden was entirely influenced by seeing it in an 'open' garden during a garden tour. I literally raced around looking for the owner to quiz what it was, then got hunting it out online. While this wasn't my first purchase inspired by the choices of others, it has been one of the most rewarding.

My two original knautia plants have matured over the last couple of years into lovely large healthy clumps. These would certainly be able to be divided to create more in the spring if I chose to.

Allowing your flowers to form seed heads in mid-autumn and allowing them to remain on the plant through early winter will encourage gentle self-seeding. You can let them naturally scatter or know that seeds are ready to harvest and save when they are dry and flaking easily off the seed head. Simply snip the whole seed head off and pop into an envelope to process when you are ready to plant in spring. Alternatively, during autumn you could help the process along by positioning seeds under a light layer of soil in the spot you would like them to grow.

If growing from seed in spring, get started undercover in seedling trays, only very lightly covering them with soil. It is always best to use a seedling specific mix to get your seeds going. Expect germination to be a little erratic, around 2–3 weeks before you see signs of growth. Move your seedlings to a larger pot around 4 weeks before graduating to the garden once they are strong and healthy with multiple sets of leaves.

Birds are your biggest threat to your baby seedlings once planted out in the garden. I'll often build a wee barrier by poking short sticks into the ground around them to protect them from being scratched out.

If you spot some potted plants for sale over the spring and summer, they will be totally fine to be planted direct in your garden.

During winter you will notice the clump leafing up with new growth around the base of your fading stalks. This would be a good time to chop back all the dying stems and growth from the previous season (if you haven't already), leaving a nice leafy mound preparing for summer. In colder climates your knautia might recede entirely to its roots – don't worry, it hasn't died on you! New growth will begin showing in early spring.

During the flowering season, regularly harvest for a vase, or snip off dying blooms before they create seed heads. This encourages the plant to continue generating new growth to create an ongoing show of flowers in your garden.

Previous page: Nothing like a quick posy on the loo! **Right:** Knautia is a beautiful airy addition to a full garden, weaving in amongst its neighbours. Pictured here planted with achillea, sweet william, *Verbena rigida* and veronicastrum.

IN THE GARDEN

Knautia adds a lovely airiness to a mixed garden bed, naturally weaving through its neighbours for a soft, casual vibe. It is a total goer and very uncomplicated, flowering from late spring right through to late autumn. This is not only extremely rewarding for your garden scape, but for all the insects interacting with it.

In spring I have the occasional self-seeded seedling appear which I can move around as I please, however by no means is it a pest with its spreading.

Knautia looks fantastic mixed in with my favourite summer flowering perennials including rudbeckia, achillea, *Verbena rigida* and echinacea. I love this flower for its low clump but mid-height flowers that bridge my other tall and short varieties surrounding it.

Top: Knautia in the foreground weaving through bed with rudbeckia, achillea, *Verbena rigida* and *Verbena bonariensis*. **Right:** Knautia in the garden. **Opposite page:** A delicate little gathering of mini chrysanthemums, lily of the valley flowers and foliage, sweet peas, heuchera flower, clover, juvenile green plum and a single sprig of knautia.

FOR THE VASE

Knautia is one of my favourite smaller flowers to add to mixed arrangements
for a dot of colour. Its long slim stems and excellent vase life make it an
incredibly handy filler flower. I particularly love adding it to mellow green and
white bunches as a disruptive pop of personality and find its 'pincushion' form
a really interesting, fun shape when paired with cosmos, dahlias and echinacea.
No special treatment required to keep it happy.

{06/12}

Bog sage

My Mum just calls this 'blue salvia' but in the world of a million salvias, this particular tall, willowy plant needs more definition. There is a kind of looseness and casual vibe to bog sage which really appeals to my love of the imperfect. Planted en masse it delivers whimsy in bucket loads. For me this is a beautiful filler plant that you could pop into gaps that need something tall behind, although it can't always be guaranteed to grow in a straight line!

Left: Bog sage, mixed with fennel, rudbeckia and Queen Anne's lace.

BOG SAGE

LATIN NAME	*Salvia uliginosa*
PLACE OF ORIGIN	Southern Brazil, Uruguay and Argentina
PLANT TYPE	Tall-growing perennial with sawtooth green leaves and elongated fuzzy head with powder blue petals. Growing to 1.5 m + tall creating clumps and slowly spreading.
FLOWERING	Summer through autumn.
GROWING CONDITIONS	Full sun and moist soil. Frost hardy.
WHEN TO PLANT	Raise seeds undercover to plant out or sow direct in position in late spring. Alternatively purchase potted up plants to transplant into garden anytime from spring to autumn. Mature plants can be divided easily to be moved in spring – this is the easiest method! Cuttings can also be made over warm months. Get good root growth started in a cup of water then transfer into small pots with potting mix before transplanting into position when healthy green growth is showing.
SPACING	50 cm +. Can be planted more sparingly as will spread over time.
WHERE TO PLANT	Back of your garden bed ideally with head in sun and feet in moist soil. By nature bog sage will slowly spread.
SUITABLE FOR CONTAINERS	Yes
PINCHING	No
CUT AND COME AGAIN	Yes
STAKING	While tempting, it is too willowy to stake easily.
SUSCEPTIBLE TO	Powdery mildew and rust.
TOXICITY	No

—How to grow—
BOG SAGE

Bog sage is a goodie for first-time gardeners. The easiest way to get it going in your garden is by planting divisions donated to you by others. Most people with bog sage will have more than enough to dig up a little for you, making it a very inexpensive way to start adding flowers to your garden. A pre-warning, it does have a slightly unusual smell!

Bog sage has a very shallow root system making it very easy to gently dig up clumps for replanting elsewhere, which is best done in early spring. With each season it slowly spreads to fill out the space provided. To divide, simply dig up smaller plants with healthy complete roots, trim off their foliage to just 15 cm or so tall and replant with water in their new position. Success can be mixed, but the majority of mine done this way have worked and begin to bush up nicely by late spring.

While it will grow in part shade, I did find that made my plants very tangled and messy, rarely growing vertically to find the sun. In a brighter position, while still very willowy and erratic, more often than not it will create an ethereal wall of leafy stems reaching to the sky.

Flowering throughout summer and into autumn, they will provide welcome green foliage in the garden until you choose to cut them back over winter. Cut back all foliage to just 15 cm high from the ground in winter. In early spring the clump will begin generating new growth and you are away again.

Previous page: Bog sage rambling in my part-shade garden. **Top:** Mature bog sage pulled out of the garden to be trimmed down and divided for replanting in the sun. **Bottom:** Bog sage gives a soft and romantic vibe as a cut flower.

IN THE GARDEN

Bog sage was the very first plant I 'introduced' to my garden as a beginner, and it was simply lined up against a shady fence. Despite it doing pretty well it was always in a tangled disarray, starved of enough sunlight to reach for the sky. I have since taken divisions and moved it to have a go in large, sunny containers. In my sister and mother's garden, as well as growing gently amongst thick planting in dappled shade, it grows beautifully tall and straight against a sunny fence, so my hopes are pinned on that result!

I simply love its fuzzy, messy elongated heads that seem to sporadically sprout perfectly blue petals. Combined with its lovely deep green foliage and long tooth-edged leaves, I feel this plant brings a romance to the garden, but also when planted en masse a kind of modern meadow vibe.

Right: A freshly picked bunch of bog sage.
Top right: Bog sage can get very wiggly when planted in part shade. It will grow straighter in direct sunlight. **Bottom right:** Bog sage with other seasonal friends including sunflowers, rudbeckia, hollyhocks and lupins.

FOR THE VASE

It's a treat to get the colour blue in your vase for a change and bog sage, with its character-filled flower heads, brings it in a kind of drunk, friendly way. Its success as a cut flower can be a little hit and miss at times, as while always surviving the first day or so it can then dramatically flop and give up.

Its appeal to me is never lessoned however, and I keep including it in the vase parties. It looks wonderful mixed with seasonal flowering friends but also fabulous as a large messed arrangement on its own.

Left: Bog sage en masse in the kitchen.
Above: A small posy including bog sage, foraged aster, oxeye daisy, common yarrow and a single 'Iceberg' rose.

Snapdragons

Romantic, frothy and straight from the pages of a fairy tale, even the name of this plant, 'snapdragon' suggests a pixie might peep from one of its bells! If you gently squeeze the throat of a flower it will appear to snap at you, hence the lovely name. I am never without snapdragons in my summer garden, dotting them through beds and planting them en masse in my cutting area. The lush look of them flowering together makes my heart beat a bit faster.

Left: The frothy joy that snapdragons bring. Plant en masse and enjoy for your garden and vase.

COMMON NAME
SNAPDRAGON or ANTIRRHINUM

LATIN NAME	*Antirrhinum majus*
PLACE OF ORIGIN	Mediterranean from southern France to Morocco, Syria and Turkey.
PLANT TYPE	Commonly grown as annuals but can behave as perennials depending on climate and variety grown. Growing from 20 cm to 1 m tall depending on variety.
FLOWERING	From late spring through summer.
GROWING CONDITIONS	Full sun to light shade.
WHEN TO PLANT	Raise seeds undercover to plant out once seedlings are strong enough with multiple sets of leaves. Wait until after frosts in late spring to plant out in the garden. Alternatively, purchase easy growing annual mixes from garden centres to pop in over spring and summer.
SPACING	15–30 cm
WHERE TO PLANT	The commonly procured annual varieties are likely only going to grow to around 30 cm which makes them perfect for the front of beds. Taller, traditional varieties can grow up to 75 cm to 1 m tall pushing them toward the middle or back. Check your labels.
SUITABLE FOR CONTAINERS	Yes
PINCHING	Yes, when it has five sets of leaves.
CUT AND COME AGAIN	Yes
STAKING	Yes, for taller varieties.
SUSCEPTIBLE TO	Rust
TOXICITY	No

—How to grow—
SNAPDRAGONS

As my gardening confidence grows, my efforts to explore a little further than my cheap punnets of snappies from the garden centre increases. However, buying the affordable packs of seedlings in wonderful, colourful mixes is such an easy and gratifying way to step into flower gardening. Not everything needs to be grown from seed... except the exquisite, old-fashioned long-stemmed varieties not readily available at garden centres.

Snapdragon seed is like dust so handle with care. Surface sprinkle your seeds into trays of seedling mix and very lightly cover with soil. You are looking at around 8–14 days for germination, then you'll need to work at caring for your seedlings until they are ready to plant out in the garden with at least three sets of leaves. You will need to protect them from birds with net or by building wee stick barriers.

Once seedlings have five sets of leaves, gently pinch out the main stem. This promotes much bushier and productive plants which will reward you with lots of flowers. You will be torn about stealing blooms for a vase because they look so lush in the garden, but regardless it is important to keep deadheading fading blooms before they set seed. This will ensure you will keep getting new flowers for as long as possible.

The main challenge I have experienced with snapdragons is the development of the fungi, rust. Rust won't necessarily kill your plants, it just reduces their general health, slows down flowering and looks yucky. The best way to manage it is keeping an eye on the foliage of your plants, snipping off any leaves that might be developing dark brown spots. Make sure you throw them in the bin, as rust is catching for other plants. Soggy weather conditions can bring it on and I have found that rust just comes part and parcel with my snapdragon crop each year. Don't stress. Alternatively you could spray with Liquid Copper (which is considered an organic treatment) if you feel it is really taking hold.

While you might be tempted to collect seed from your store-bought shorter plants, it is often likely that they will be sterile. The taller, old-fashioned varieties however offer potential for self-seeding if you can handle that dust!

Previous page: The top tier of my stacked vegetable garden has been confiscated to be my cutting garden. **Right:** Vibrant plump snapdragons being gathered up for an arrangement inside.

MY FAVOURITES

To give snapdragons a fast easy test run in your garden, I would highly advise picking up cheap and cheerful mixes in punnets from a hardware store or garden centre. This will help you find your love for them. You would mostly pick these up in late spring/summer and I'd recommend looking out for the Bubblegum mixes for full frothy colour which grow to around 45 cm. On these same garden centre tables you will see other offerings that might interest you, but always check expected height on the labels.

If you want to venture to loftier heights, look for seeds of the Madame Butterfly and Chantilly varieties. There are some total beauties out there that I covet including 'Madame Butterfly Red', 'Madame Butterfly Bronze' and 'Potomac Orange' that will grow to a metre!

IN THE GARDEN

Their plump and romantic spires are a wonderful addition to your mix of garden shapes, not to mention all the choice they provide for adding punctuating colour. As mentioned, I tend to grow them en masse in my cutting garden (aka part of my vege garden) which is incredibly pleasing to see in full flower. This means I am replanting each year in a space that I clear of leftover winter veg. It's my hope as I collect taller, old-fashioned varieties that I might have some luck encouraging self-seeding or hopefully they might even perennialise! Nonetheless, they bring an abundance and cheerfulness to my garden that I always appreciate.

Left: A simple few stems on the windowsill in the kitchen bring instant brightening to the day.
Below: Snapdragons are best picked when only the bottom few petals have opened. The rest will slowly come out in the vase.

FOR THE VASE

Some might find the shorter varieties a little tricker to pick for arrangements as the pickable stem is often quite short in relation to the bloom, but as a home arranger, it's not really a big deal. Just create smaller arrangements.

For best results, when choosing blooms to harvest, aim for ones that only have around two to four of the bottom flowers open. The rest will slowly open in the vase which is glorious!

When cutting you want to snip the flower stem on an angle, above a leaf node or branch intersection. This encourages new growth which you'll want later in the season. As soon as possible strip off all the leaves that you think will be below water level in your vase and promptly sink into some water while you prepare your vessel and other stems. Give them a second quick snip as you place into your arrangement and don't forget to regularly top up and change their water to prolong vase life.

Their beauty is such that a single snapdragon spire in a bottle is just as appealing as adding them into mixed arrangements. There is something about deeply saturated snap petals supporting looser, more delicate blooms around them.

Above: A vibrant bunch of summery pinks from the garden featuring snapdragons with cosmos, echinacea, thalictrum, *Sanguisorba obtusa*, *Verbena rigida* and a large dahlia.
Next page: I have annexed the top tier of my stacked vegetable garden to act as a cutting garden that I can readily snip which reduces the impact of cutting on my garden beds.

I am never without snapdragons in my summer garden, dotting them through beds and planting them en masse in my cutting area. The lush look of them flowering together makes my heart beat a bit faster.

Echinacea

Echinacea is like the happy, easy-going clown of my garden who just wants to hang around for as long as possible. Collecting different varieties of echinacea has become a bit of a 'thing' for me. In all honesty, beyond knowing it was good in pill form to ward off colds, I really had no idea that it was actually an interesting, cartoonish addition to my perennial flower garden. Now I am hooked.

Left: *Echinacea purpurea* 'Baby Swan White' with dahlias, spring onion flower, chocolate cosmos, petunias, snapdragon, sweet peas, mint and scabiosa.

ECHINACEA or CONEFLOWER

LATIN NAME	The *Echinacea* genus with our focus being on *Echinacea angustifolia*, *Echinacea purpurea* and *Echinacea pallida*.
PLACE OF ORIGIN	Eastern and central North America
PLANT TYPE	Perennial growing 50 cm and up to 1.2 m tall depending on species. Dies back to roots only over winter.
FLOWERING	Summer through autumn.
GROWING CONDITIONS	Full sun and part shade. Well-drained soil.
WHEN TO PLANT	Raise seeds undercover to plant out or sow direct in position in early summer. Alternatively purchase potted up plants. Divide mature plants after three or more years in early spring.
SPACING	Approx. 20 cm for a nice full looking garden.
WHERE TO PLANT	Depending on the specific variety you buy, they can be great additions for front, mid and back of your mixed garden beds.
SUITABLE FOR CONTAINERS	Yes
PINCHING	No
CUT AND COME AGAIN	Yes
STAKING	No
SUSCEPTIBLE TO	Occasional powdery mildew.
TOXICITY	No but if you intend to harvest *Echinacea purpurea* for its health benefits, please do comprehensive research first.

—How to grow—
ECHINACEA

The good news is that in general, echinacea is a very uncomplicated and rewarding plant. I have raised from seed and transplanted throughout the garden where healthy two- to three-year-old clumps have now matured. My first echinacea was bought as an experiment from the perennials table at my local garden centre, which provided a fast, gratifying introduction to growing it.

Sow seeds undercover 8–10 weeks before planting out seedlings in the garden in early summer onwards. Purchased plants can go in at any point of summer to early autumn as you come across them for sale, just remember that they will die back over winter and not to fret!

As a prairie plant it is more tolerant of dry spells than others and I have noticed that it still performs well in my dappled shade areas. Plants in their second season and beyond are terrifically satisfying bloomers and attract a lot of attention from pollinators.

Picking and deadheading will encourage the plant to keep producing flowers until autumn. The great graphic shape of their cone seed heads are lovely to then leave to mature on the plant, offering a nibble for birds and a subtle chance of self-seeding. I don't find them invasive and in spring often prick out surrounding seedlings to plant elsewhere in the garden.

To test if seed heads are ready to be harvested to save, gently run your thumb over the top. It is ready to be snipped off if the seeds easily come away from the centre.

In winter cut down the plant to the ground where it will recede to its roots, with new growth showing in early spring.

Previous page: 'Baby Swan White' and classic pink *Echinacea purpurea* standing guard in the garden. **Right:** A bumblebee with *Echinacea purpurea* alongside astrantia, pompom dahlia, snapdragons, fuchsia, achillea, Iceland poppies and larkspur.

MY FAVOURITES

For your first foray, look for classic *Echinacea purpurea* with its recognisable coneflower shape and lipstick pink-coloured petals. I have really enjoyed growing my pinks alongside whites with 'Baby Swan White' (growing to 50 cm) and 'Alba' (growing up to 1.2 m). For a weirder and wonderful look, seek out the 'Doubledecker' variety that has a secondary bloom coming out of the top of the cone or multi-coloured 'Giant Lime' which mixes green through the pink petals. For acid brights look for 'Cheyenne Spirit' with its electric coral-coloured blooms.

For the longer, droopier petaled look, search around for varieties of *Echinacea pallida* and *Echinacea angustifolia* with its narrow petals.

IN THE GARDEN

As one of my first flowering summer perennials that I bought (knowing nothing much at all) it has been a real cheerleader of a plant. Uncomplicated in care and very rewarding in appearance in the garden, mixed in with all sorts of friends. I've really enjoyed its form grown alongside lacier plants such as sanguisorba and its prairie cousins, rudbeckia. It is also a real star of the 'naturalistic' planting style and is fabulous amid misty grasses.

This is also a plant that will reward your winter garden if you choose to leave seed heads on. The little remaining ball-shaped seed heads are a wonderful snack for birds and provide an architectural interest.

Clockwise from above: 'Cheyenne Spirit'; *Echinacea angustifolia*; *Echinacea purpurea*; 'Giant Lime'.

Echinacea is like the happy, easy-going clown of my garden who just wants to hang around for as long as possible.

Right: *Echinacea angustifolia* and 'Baby Swan White' with a big bright dahlia, astrantia, *Verbena bonariensis, Verbena rigida,* Queen Anne's Lace, scabiosa, thalictrum, oregano flower and *Sanguisorba obtusa.* **Next page:** Rudbeckia in a large casual bunch in my studio with asters, bog sage and lupins.

FOR THE VASE

This is a high performer for the vase and
a bit of a showstopper with its quirky, fun
form. Echinacea has long smooth stems
which make it very friendly when you are
sliding it into an arrangement.

When the petals begin to wilt and die I
pluck them off and reuse the glossy round
seed head centres in posies. This provides
a really unexpected shape in a bunch and
also great longevity and use of the plant.

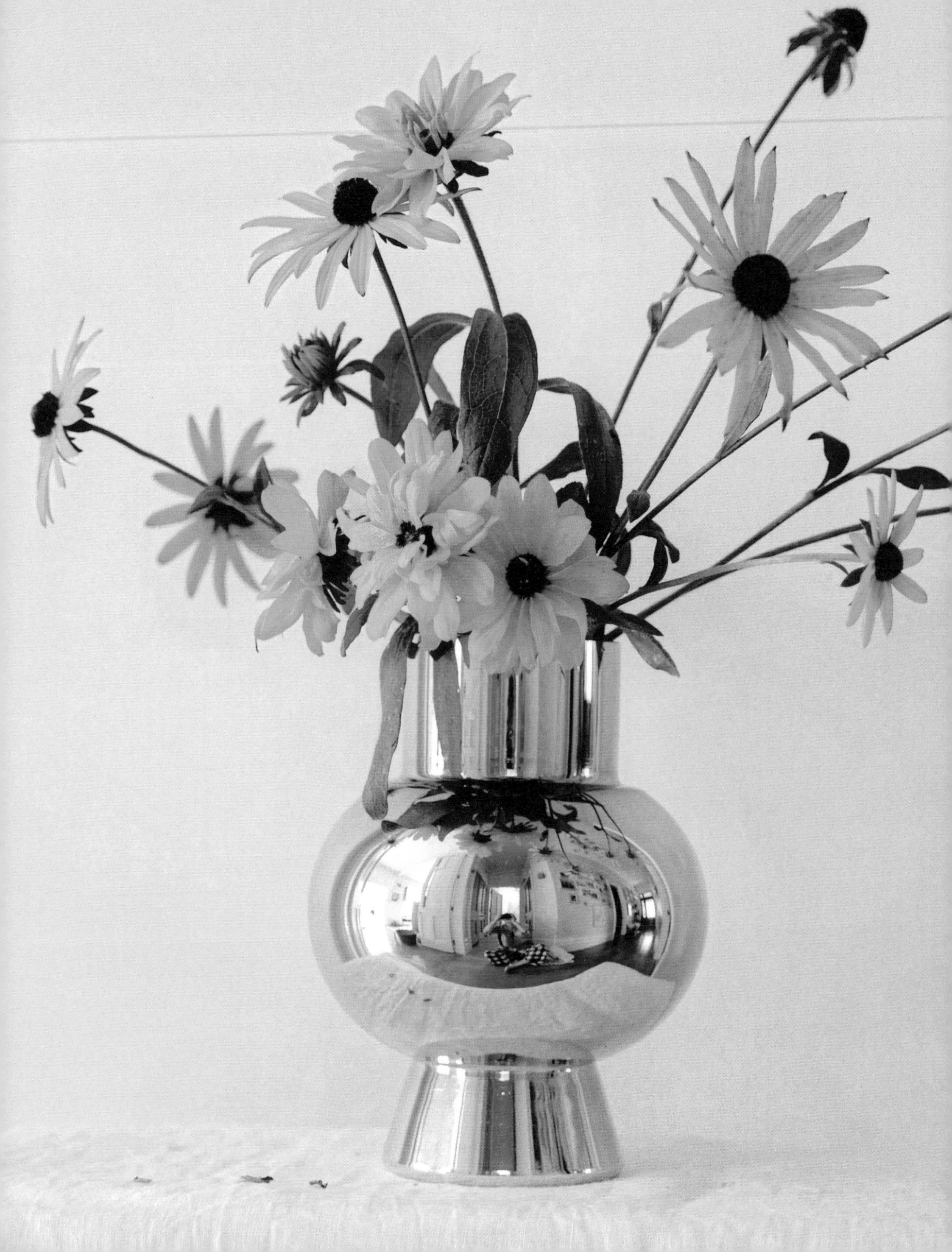

{09/12}

Rudbeckia

I can say, with hand on heart, that I never set out to populate my garden with orangey yellow flowers. Orange and yellow are very low on my list of tolerable colours but, as with all things in my life, gardening has changed that. While they will never venture into my house via paint or homeware, colour from Mother Nature is simply different and rudbeckia is now a full-blown obsession for me.

Left: A sunny mix of rudbeckia from the garden.

RUDBECKIA, BLACK-EYED SUSAN or CONEFLOWER

LATIN NAME	*Rudbeckia* species with an emphasis on *Rudbeckia hirta* and perennial cultivars.
PLACE OF ORIGIN	North America
PLANT TYPE	Clump-forming perennials with annual varieties too. Growing between 40 cm and 2 m depending on variety.
FLOWERING	Summer through autumn.
GROWING CONDITIONS	Full sun but will tolerate light shade.
WHEN TO PLANT	Raise from seed undercover in spring to plant out after risk of frost has passed. Purchased perennial plants can be planted at any time from spring to autumn. Divide clumps in early spring.
SPACING	Approx. 20 cm for dwarf varieties and 50 cm for taller ones.
WHERE TO PLANT	Depending on your variety from the front to the back of the garden bed.
SUITABLE FOR CONTAINERS	Yes
PINCHING	No
CUT AND COME AGAIN	Yes
STAKING	No
SUSCEPTIBLE TO	Occasional powdery mildew.
TOXICITY	Yes, if large amounts are eaten by humans or pets.

Clockwise from top: Rudbeckia and fennel being harvested for an arrangement; *Rudbeckia* 'Goldsturm' piled in with bog sage; nasturtium flower and *Sanguisorba obtusa.*

—How to grow—
RUDBECKIA

I think the biggest trick when delving into the world of rudbeckia is identifying if you are planting an annual or a perennial. The majority of mine are perennials which I far prefer, allowing them to establish over time and divide when I want more plants, however the annual varieties tend to be the shorter ones which are cool for pots and filling in edges near the front of a garden bed. So research or read the labels when purchasing plants or seed.

Growing them from seed is a mostly straightforward activity. I've only stumbled across issues one year when they didn't germinate for months and then I ended up with bizarre miniature versions, as well as an imposter species that wasn't invited. I have a feeling this was due to keeping my seed trays too wet. Yet another reminder that gardening is not an exact science! Grow them in early spring to plant out in late spring or early summer.

Rudbeckia is yet to be a mainstream garden centre plant so I would recommend exploring the options of plant purchases through specialty perennial nurseries and even online trading platforms.

It is a great plant to be actively picking for the vase, or deadheading to encourage fresh growth as the plant slows down if it forms seed heads. I leave my flowers to form seed heads when I start to notice the leaves looking a little tired. The interest provided by the bobble-headed stems is welcome visually but also for birds hunting for lunch in the winter months.

To harvest your own seed, gently run your thumb over the seed head. If the spikes of seeds easily pull away you are good to go. If not, they need a little more time on the plant.

In winter I trim the plant down close to the ground or to the new foliage growth developing on the clump. If it is an annual, I simply pull it out.

Right: I never set out to have bright yellow flowers in my garden, but thoroughly enjoy their graphic, punchy vibe weaving through others as seen here with *Rudbeckia* 'Goldsturm', *Verbena rigida* and *Knautia macedonica*.

MY FAVOURITES

My favourite rudbeckia was picked up for $5 off the Christchurch Botanic Gardens seedling table and sadly, with no name! On research I am quite sure it is *Rudbeckia* 'Goldsturm'. I'm also encouraging *Rudbeckia hirta* 'Irish Eyes' with lovely pale green centres and yellow petals, although the jury is out if it is an annual or short-lived perennial.

   I would love to get my hands on *Rudbeckia laciniata* 'Herbstsonne' with its pronounced cones, yellow petals that fall from the centre and incredible scopey height of 2 m! *Rudbeckia amplexicaulis* 'Clasping Coneflower' is another I would love to establish with self-seeding. A terrific and punchy annual option would be any of the cultivars of *Rudbeckia hirta,* which tend to be shorter and have hairy stems. I've hosted many and they are all great.

IN THE GARDEN

Once I got over my discrimination of yellow in the garden I was rewarded with the playful, graphic vibe that rudbeckia brings. My perennial patches are so satisfying, requiring minimum attention for maximum, positive impact. The perennial varieties I have are lovely and loose on long stalks, weaving between their neighbours like *Knautia macedonica* and *Verbena rigida*. Plants like these encourage the feeling of a messy, mixed arrangement in the ground which I just love. I am very interested in introducing more of the green-centred varieties as they have a slightly softer vibe than the bold, dark dots of the others.

With cutting for the vase and diligent deadheading, my perennial rudbeckias will flower from summer, right through autumn. As the plants start to look a little tired I then allow seed heads to form for collection. The seed heads also provide an interesting visual effect within the garden. When I cut them back in winter, it is only to reveal all the new green growth of the clump which remains throughout winter, acting as a bit of a green island in my otherwise bare perennial patch!

Clockwise from left: *Rudbeckia hirta* flowers that have sprouted a few extra petals from the centre mixed with garden bruised *Rudbeckia* 'Goldsturm'; 'Irish Eyes' with its lovely soft green centre; annual *Rudbeckia hirta* in a pot; *Rudbeckia* 'Goldsturm' floating in the garden with *Verbena rigida*.

Left: A mix of merry rudbeckia.
Right: Rudbeckia in a large casual bunch in my studio with asters, bog sage and lupins.
Next page: A late autumn clean-up on a crisp morning.

FOR THE VASE

This is another really trustworthy cut flower for you to play with. Beyond the dwarf varieties, you are rewarded with brilliant long smooth stems which allows them to easily slip into a mixed arrangement. Their colour means it's hard for them to not be the statement in a vase, but their lovely fun shape makes this all well worth it.

When harvesting, make an effort to cut each bloom's stem as close to the main stem as possible to encourage new growth. I have found all rudbeckia (perennial or annual) to have incredibly long vase life and often move them to a new vase once all their friends have finished.

Cosmos

Once you have cosmos in your garden, you won't want to do without it. It brings a rambling, wild lightness, greeting you with sunny faces and delicate, long winding stems amid light ferny foliage. There are lots of beautiful and novel varieties to be explored, and providing you can give them a sunny spot and a gentle deadhead when needed, they will flower and flower until the frosts hit.

Left: Cosmos with Japanese anemones, gomphrena, snapdragons, lupin, *Knautia macedonica*, achillea and *Verbena bonariensis*.

COMMON NAME
COSMOS

LATIN NAME	*Cosmos bipinnatus*
PLACE OF ORIGIN	Mexico, United States, Central and South America.
PLANT TYPE	Half-Hardy annual growing up to approx. 120 cm or dwarf varieties around 60 cm.
FLOWERING	Summer through to autumn frosts.
GROWING CONDITIONS	Full sun.
WHEN TO PLANT	Sow direct early summer. Alternatively raise undercover to plant out late spring/early summer. Transfer purchased punnets of seedlings late spring/early summer.
SPACING	30 cm
WHERE TO PLANT	Tall plants in mid or back of garden bed. Dwarf plants along front.
SUITABLE FOR CONTAINERS	Yes
PINCHING	Yes
CUT AND COME AGAIN	Yes
STAKING	Yes for tall plants, not supported in mass planting.
SUSCEPTIBLE TO	Powdery mildew
TOXICITY	No

—How to grow—
COSMOS

Easily cultivated from seed, cosmos is also a good self-seeder without being invasive. Punnets of cheerful healthy seedlings can also be purchased in spring to easily plant out directly into the garden. Alternatively, you could sow seeds direct in the ground in New Zealand from early summer or raise seedlings undercover from mid-spring, planting out in late spring/early summer.

Once seedlings develop 2–3 pairs of leaves, pinch out the growing tips to encourage a bushier plant. This seems scary but you will be on the receiving end of triple the blooms! A step that is often forgotten by many but reaps the rewards. A healthy plant with good sunlight exposure will mature into a bushy base with large daisy-like flowers on long slim stems and fern-like leaves.

To harvest for your vase or encourage endless flowering until the first frosts, simply snip off spent flowers close to where they meet the stalk. The removing of the flower (a potential seed head the plant is aiming to grow) encourages new growth to develop from just above that intersection as the plant attempts to produce more.

Tall plants can get top-heavy and may need staking for support. It is best to put your stakes in when the plant is just a seedling to avoid damaging roots later; after the fact will still work, just be gentle! It's a sad day seeing your prize cosmos plant lying flat after a blustery front comes through.

As the season cools, halt deadheading and let your flowers go to seed in early autumn. Allow them to dry completely on the plant before either snipping off heads to store in a dry envelope or scattering in position to encourage a nice self-seeded crop next year. I prefer self-seeded plants that I like and can edit back rather than bare earth for unwanted weeds to take over.

Like sweet peas, cosmos is susceptible to powdery mildew often triggered by the stress of underwatering or lack of air circulation. I often notice it arriving at the end of the plant's natural life cycle. Once plants look like they are dying simply pull out from the roots and throw in the compost/green bin, leaving that part of your garden clear for self-seeded seedlings in spring or whatever else you choose to plant!

Previous page: *Cosmos* 'Sonata' in pinks and whites mixed in a border with snapdragons, petunias, Queen Anne's lace and gypsophila. **Top right:** Just-picked *Cosmos* 'Cupcake' with *Scabiosa* 'Fama White', cornflowers, Iceland poppies, Japanese anemones, lupins, dahlias and veronica. **Bottom right:** *Cosmos* 'Cupcake' with fennel, achillea, Iceland poppies and rudbeckia.

Clockwise from left:
Perfect *Cosmos* 'Sonata'; the
incredible fused petals of *Cosmos*
'Cupcake'; seed packs will always
bring surprises with speckled
or even vivid variation like the
Cosmos 'Cupcake'; a pretty pale
pink *Cosmos* 'Cupcake'.

MY FAVOURITES

For your classic cosmos form, look for readily available
seedling punnets of 'Sonata' in white and pink from garden
centres. Just be sure you identify them as dwarf or tall!

As eager strong germinators, they are fun to grow from
seed so look out for 'Seashell' mixes with crazy, fluted petals
and 'Cupcake' which astonishingly looks like paper cupcake
wrappers. For richness in colour find 'Rubenza' or soft yellow
tones in 'Apricot Lemonade'. 'Double Click' is a must for those
seeking the impossibly frou-frou blooms.

IN THE GARDEN

Tall cosmos looks amazing weaving up through other plants, as much as it does planted en masse.

More is more when it comes to this plant, so don't skimp! You will want to have plenty so that you can cut for inside, without ruining your garden scape.

I love it so much that I plant it both in my cutting garden area as well as purposefully leaving pockets of space to replant each year among my flowering perennials. Its light lacy foliage and variety of interesting colours add an ethereal quality to a garden bed. I have found that they will cope with dappled shade, so it's always worth a go if that is the only space you have.

FOR THE VASE

Cosmos are long-lasting cut flowers that give a lovely casual romance to all bunches. They look amazing gathered en masse with their lacy foliage as much as weaving through a mix of their seasonal friends. As the season progresses you will find that their stems get shorter, but that will just push you to get creative or very bold and harvest whole branches for a wild look.

Trim off foliage below water line to help prevent bacteria degrading your vase water. Check and top up water daily for best results.

Left: An end-of-season clutch of happy pink cosmos. Specific variety unknown. **Above:** Soft pink and white *Cosmos* 'Cupcake' with some double petaled variation mixed casually with fennel, Queen Anne's lace, snapdragon, lupins and Shasta daisy.

Cosmos are long-lasting cut flowers that give a lovely casual romance to all bunches. They look amazing gathered en masse with their lacy foliage as much as weaving through a mix of their seasonal friends.

Right: Pink *Cosmos* 'Sonata' mixed with a wild bunch of seasonal, early autumn friends including nasturtium foliage, lupins, nemesia, penstemon, 'Iceberg' rose and hips, hollyhock, *Knautia macedonica* and rudbeckia. **Next page:** White *Cosmos* 'Sonata' in a romantic bunch with bog sage, pink and white Japanese anemones plus seed heads, nemesia, mint flower, fennel, aster and clematis.

Dahlias

For me, fresh to flower gardening, dahlias were a kind of rite of passage.
After I had played around with fun annuals, then dipped a toe in
uncomplicated perennials, dahlias not only demanded a little more
attention in their preparation and care but rewarded me with the most
impressive blooms. Your first flowering dahlia will leave you feeling a little
like you're starting to know what you are doing.

Left: A weird and wonderful gathering with *Dahlia* 'Shiloh Noelle', *Cosmos* 'Cupcake', veronica, echinacea, rudbeckia,
snapdragons, lupin and a white single dahlia peeping out at the top.

COMMON NAME

DAHLIA

LATIN NAME	*Dahlia* (with many species)
PLACE OF ORIGIN	Mexico and Central America
PLANT TYPE	Bushy perennial grown from seed or tuber. Depending on variety will grow from 50 cm to 1 m +.
FLOWERING	Mid-summer to autumn frosts.
GROWING CONDITIONS	Full sun
WHEN TO PLANT	Very cold and frost sensitive so beware. Raise seeds undercover to plant out or sow direct in position in mid/late spring after the frosts. It is most common to purchase tubers to plant out in mid/late spring.
SPACING	45–60 cm. Depending on variety, many mature to be very bushy.
WHERE TO PLANT	Depending on variety, mid to back of sunny garden bed. Plant dwarf at front.
SUITABLE FOR CONTAINERS	Yes
PINCHING	Yes
CUT AND COME AGAIN	Yes
STAKING	Yes, for tall plants when not supported in mass planting.
SUSCEPTIBLE TO	Powdery mildew, tuber rot, blight, slugs and snails. Earwigs like to live in their blooms.
TOXICITY	Yes, mildly poisonous if leaves ingested by dogs, cats or horses.

—How to grow—
DAHLIAS

Don't be concerned that dahlias demand a little extra care. Once established in happy spots they are so rewarding it is worth increasing your knowledge for. Dahlias come in a huge and endless rainbow of colours and species. These are mostly identified by the form of their blooms and include cactus, decorative, pompom, ball, anemone, collarette, single, peony, orchid, waterlily and dinner plate among other subspecies. Within these species there are variations in not only colour, but foliage, stem colour and expected height of maturity. It is a really exciting thing to trawl dahlia catalogues to make your choice!

Dahlias need a sunny spot, with dappled shade at the very most. They also have brittle stems and limbs that may well need support as they mature. Large blooming varieties will bend and snap under the weight of their flowers.

Before you plant your tubers or transfer plants, place your stakes or supports in the ground first to avoid damaging tubers later on. I've used wooden stakes in the past and more recently have bought circular steel supports that they will grow up through.

Dahlia seeds are very thin and flat so only need to be sown just below the surface in your seed tray. Resist transplanting your seedlings into the garden until they have a strong set of leaves and the frosts are well gone.

Dahlias are most commonly grown by purchasing, being given or dividing tubers. Tubers are weird-looking storage organs that not only deliver you a flowering plant in their first season, but also readily multiply to be dug up and divided to create more plants in the future.

If you order or purchase dahlias they will either come as a small gathering of tubers around a cut-off stem or as single tubers of which each will have an 'eye'. A tuber without an eye will not grow, so this is something to bear in mind when you are dividing your clumps in the future.

The eye is identified as a small bump at the end of the tuber, where a stem may have sprouted and mostly at the opposite end to any roots that may be attached. This is the only area that an eye can form, so if you damage these during division, just throw the eyeless tubers away. If in doubt, a quick search online will bring up some fabulous videos clearly demonstrating what you are looking for.

Plant your dahlias only after you feel you are well clear of frosts in your area. Their new growth is really tender and will die if frosted. To plant, lie your tuber horizontally with the eye facing upward in a hole around 10–15 cm deep.

Previous page: 'Shiloh Noelle' alongside 'Rococo' pompom dahlia. These do really well in containers with diligent watering and deadheading to prolong the flowering period. **Right:** A fun little arrangement with 'Rococo' pompom dahlias, strawberries and their foliage, sedum, snapdragons and clematis.

Your first flowering dahlia will leave you feeling a little like you're starting to know what you are doing.

They don't require regular watering until you see the first wee green shoot pushing through the soil. Then it's important to give them deep soaks a couple of times a week.

Once your plant has four sets of leaves or is approximately 30 cm tall, you want to 'pinch' the central stem off. Using some sharp snips, cut the stem closely between the fourth set of leaves or, if working on height, take out around 10 cm of growth from the top. This seems scary but will encourage the plant to bush up and dramatically reward you with more blooms later on. Don't fret if you don't get to them soon enough, even if your young plant has grown taller, it is still worth doing. Pinching is particularly beneficial for smaller, weaker stemmed varieties.

Dahlias grown from seed can take longer to mature and produce lots of blooms, however it is a great affordable way to get lots of dahlia plants. Growing from seed also means your plants may not always resemble the ones you have collected them from! In fact you may get different colours and shapes from a single seed pod. After the first season flowering, you can then dig up and divide the tuber clumps of your seed-grown dahlias, knowing that the ones you choose to plant will look like its mother.

To make the most of your dahlia plants, dedicate yourself to picking for a vase or deadheading spent flowers during the season. Removing them before they form seed heads will encourage your plant to keep producing. Do this by cutting the flower and its stem off right near the point it meets the main stem. It is from that wee intersection that a new stem will form.

In late autumn, with the arrival of frosts, your plant will slowly start 'putting itself to bed'. No longer blooming, leaves will start to die back and you should let them do so before pruning completely for winter. The clump needs to feed off its wilting foliage, so wait a few weeks to then simply cut off all stems close to the ground.

TO LIFT OR TO LEAVE

In colder climates that experience months of snow like North America, it is common for gardeners to gently dig up and 'lift' their dahlia clumps, washing off all dirt before letting them dry and storing them in a dry dark place over winter, often in sawdust. In spring, before planting they will divide these clumps to create new plants which they can sell, give away or replant.

The jury is still out for me here in coastal Canterbury. I have lifted clumps over winter to divide then replanted with success. I have also left them in the ground with a nice thick layer of mulch over the crowns of the clumps which I dust off in early spring. Both have worked well, however I did lose some to rot during a particularly wet winter. The best I can advise you is to ask around locally. This guidance, relevant to your immediate climate, will be most rewarding to your success of growing dahlias year after year.

Regardless of whether you choose to lift or leave your dahlias, it is a good idea to dig up and divide every few years. You will be amazed at the multiplication of tubers below ground level! Dividing is good for both increasing your stock of that plant at no cost, but also large undivided clumps can be prone to rot if left in the ground.

Dividing is not nearly as intimidating as it sounds and this is where the internet is very much your friend. Armed with my phone I carefully snip through my clumps, removing small or damaged tubers and identifying healthy ones with an eye, all the while kept in good company by a YouTube garden expert doing the same.

MY FAVOURITES

The first dahlias I ever planted are still my
favourites. Tall-growing pompom 'Rococo' with its
deep crimson balls and ridiculously lush 'Shiloh
Noelle' with her huge blooms, a blush centre
and creamy petals. 'Shiloh Noelle' is a decorative
dahlia that feels like an interesting alternative to
every florist's favourite 'Café Au Lait'. Welcome the
wild lucky dips you get from tubers gifted from
other gardeners. I particularly love the singles
and random decorative types that I have been
given with no names to refer on to you. Quiz your
benefactor on their height so you know where to
plant but simply be prepared for some splendour!

Previous page: Little white dahlia with sea holly and the strange seed pods of love-in-a-mist. **Clockwise from right:** My first dahlia I grew; dahlias with lupins, hollyhocks, nemesia and achillea; a freshly opened 'Shiloh Noelle' with her beautiful graduated colour.

IN THE GARDEN

Dahlias bring the artistry. No matter the variety of blooms you grow, your flowering dahlias will provide a focal and talking point for garden wanders. I feel I started my collection with conservative varieties, however, with each season of enjoying their show in the garden and in arrangements, I now lust for the weird and wacky.

Dahlias look fantastic dotted throughout a full garden and work well grown with bearded irises – the irises blooming in spring while the dahlias are just emerging, and the dahlias taking up the space in summer. There is also nothing quite as decadent as dahlias planted en masse with no regard to colour, simply a chorus of the bright and cheerful. Visit your local botanical gardens as they might have a display like this in late summer.

I have successfully grown my dahlias in pots as well as garden beds. A sunny aspect is the key and watering is even more important for containers during the hot dry months.

FOR THE VASE

You will no doubt become a dahlia watcher, noticing as your buds begin to bloom and which you might leave and which you might cut for the vase. Dahlia blooms have the best chance at a good vase life when you pick them just as they have opened fully. By picking across the varieties you will ensure that you have lots of juicy shapes and colours to choose from for your arrangements.

Left: Various unnamed 'single' and pompom dahlias given to me as tubers by my mum, mixed in with lupins and hollyhocks. **Above:** A hurried little collection including 'Shiloh Noelle', scabiosa, lupin, foxglove, fennel and parsley flower. **Next page:** 'Rococo' pompom dahlia thriving in mid-summer; a little collection of 'Rococo', fennel and rudbeckia for my desk.

{12/12}

Japanese anemones

Just when you feel a bit sad about the end of summer, the happy faces of Japanese anemones rescue you and your garden. For me they are endlessly satisfying both in the garden and for the vase, adding interest with their long stems emerging from broad, leafy clumps. They come with an inbuilt cheeriness.

Left: White and pink Japanese anemones with *Verbena bonariensis*, foxgloves, hollyhocks, fennel, aquilegia foliage and a raspberry cane.

JAPANESE ANEMONE or WINDFLOWER

LATIN NAME	*Anemone hupehensis*
PLACE OF ORIGIN	Central China
PLANT TYPE	Clump-forming, spreading perennial available with pink and white flowers, growing between 60 cm to 1.2 m. Thrives in part shade.
FLOWERING	Late summer through autumn.
GROWING CONDITIONS	Part shade to sun. If in full sun, need moist soil. If too shady, flower stems will grow leggy and flop over.
WHEN TO PLANT	Rarely raised from seed due to all being hybrids. This means they will not grow true to their original plant if grown from seed. Easiest and best practice to purchase potted up plants, take root cuttings or clump divisions in winter or early spring.
SPACING	60 cm +
WHERE TO PLANT	Very handy for shady areas or large empty spaces you would like to fill, as they readily spread. Middle to back of border.
SUITABLE FOR CONTAINERS	Yes, large containers only.
PINCHING	No
CUT AND COME AGAIN	No
STAKING	Yes, if very tall they tend to flop.
SUSCEPTIBLE TO	Largely free of issues.
TOXICITY	Yes, if large amounts are eaten by humans or pets.

—How to grow—
JAPANESE ANEMONES

The fastest and easiest way to establish Japanese anemones in your garden is by planting divisions or root cuttings. Japanese anemones take around two years to really establish and it is then that you will notice not only that the main clump will increase in size but that it will shoot out runners which are forming new small plants away from the original. It's these that can be very easily lifted and relocated as you please. After replanting these babies, they will look as if they are dead, but it won't be long until you see new green shoots emerging as they really are tough and eager growers. Plant around 60 cm apart as they will certainly claim their space.

Alternatively, if you are after a large haul at minimal cost, you could propagate using root cuttings. This is done by digging up a clump and separating off strong healthy roots, snipping them into approximately 10 cm sections. Ideally you will be able to identify small nodules along the root which are essentially a new plant each. Lay these cuttings horizontally in a tray of moist potting mix and cover lightly with a few centimetres of soil, nodules facing upward. Monitor to keep moist and new shoots will appear over a couple of weeks. Plant out healthy seedlings in late spring after risk of frost.

After flowering, I allow my plants to form their attractive seed heads and cut the entire plant down to around 20 cm above the ground in winter, from where it will regenerate with lush healthy foliage in the spring, preparing for late summer flowering.

Previous page: Pink Japanese anemones bringing the happy vibes to my autumn garden. **Right:** White Japanese anemones in a casual gathering in the kitchen with bog sage and rudbeckia.

MY FAVOURITES

There are so many variations of Japanese anemone out there and due to mine being 'thieved' I don't know exactly what they are. I believe my white one is *Anemone x hybrida* 'White', and my pink one perhaps the same. However, with a little research you will see there are some fabulous deeper pinks and double blooms out there. Have some fun!

IN THE GARDEN

The first mention of introducing Japanese anemones to your garden will yield lots of warnings of their invasiveness. Sure, if you establish a patch and want to be entirely rid of it, it might take a while to dig out all the clumps, but I welcome its obvious filling out and spreading in my own garden.

With half of my own plot in part to full shade, I struggle to find flowering plants that I like to survive and thrive in those areas. That was until I met Japanese anemones.

Introduced to my own garden by simply plucking out runners from my mum's garden, I now have two beautifully established patches that I both monitor and encourage. I pluck out runners when they are heading in the 'wrong' direction and replant down the bed where I would appreciate their personality. Currently I have a patch of pinks and a patch of whites balancing each side of the garden; I enjoy their separation.

As the season cools off and the petals begin to drop, the plants move into a new phase of interest. Little spherical seed heads remain, giving a really interesting architecture to the garden. As they mature they seem to fracture and burst to reveal cotton wool type seeds that look incredible floating around their heads and drifting off around the garden.

Above top and bottom: Locating a runner to pull out and replant elsewhere in the garden.
Opposite page: Top: Japanese anemones are the welcome surprise after your summer flowering plants start to fade. **Bottom left:** The 'nude' seed heads after the petals have fallen off are still magical in both the garden and vase. **Bottom right:** Rescuing a broken stem.

Left: A single pink Japanese anemone with velvety friends including pompom dahlias, pansies, snapdragons, sweet peas, *Verbena bonariensis*, echinacea, gomphrena, oregano and mint flowers. **Above:** A romantic bunch with Japanese anemones and seed heads, mint flowers, bog sage, nemesia, asters, clematis, oregano, fennel and lupins. **Next page:** Even as they move through their season, Japanese anemones still bring interest from their buds, blooms and sweet ball-like seed heads. These eventually burst into clouds of cotton wool.

FOR THE VASE

Japanese anemones are totally glorious cut flowers! Every piece of them in fact. Their lovely long stems allow you to scale up your normal arrangements and they have a terrific vase life. Don't overlook their lush foliage to make use of, and I am super fond of their little ball-like seed heads that get revealed when the petals drop.

Often I am able to graduate the stems that have long since lost their petals in one arrangement into another, as well as simply allowing them to dry standing in a vase, giving me an arrangement through the winter months. They are such a terrific shape!

GARDEN TO VASE

Growing up it was the norm to have a little vase of pickings at our bedsides. The kitchen table looked nude without a mixed posy of mum's seasonal flowers taking up their permanent coaster. As a new gardener I've found home-grown flowers on display to be casual, sentimental and friendly, pulling what is going on outside, indoors to your daily life. This chapter offers you my tips and tricks to inspire you to enjoy your seasonal blooms too.

—Harvesting your own—
FLOWERS

My pathway to growing a garden was inspired by the promise of picking for my own spaces, providing a gateway and motivation to learn how to grow my own soul food. It's an uncomplicated activity that offers a reprieve in a busy day and a distraction for a busy mind. The growing of soul food as opposed to actual 'food', is a different but worthy addition to your wellbeing.

Abundant stems of flowers in the garden are equally enjoyable in a vase, yet filling your home with flowers undoubtedly causes an aesthetic blow to the beds they came from. Harvesting for the vase ultimately takes away from the atmosphere you have cultivated in your garden, but there are ways to reduce the impact.

One option is to nominate a bed as a cutting garden. A space you can rampage through with your snips, without pillaging your general garden scape. A second alternative is taking the time to nibble blooms from the back of the plant and from spots with less visual impact. Sometimes I'll even wait until I know a flower has only days left of being at its best, before snipping it off and popping it into a short-lived arrangement. Getting the best of it for both inside and out.

VASES AND SUPPORT

Anything goes when it comes to vases: glasses, mugs, jugs, jars, bottles, any watertight vessel! Part of the fun and creativity of displaying your flowers is to play around with what they are in. Vessels with narrow tops are handy for supporting stems however you can't fit as many in. Wide openings present a new challenge as they remove a lot of support but, in my eyes, open up the potential for that lovely rambling vibe.

Remember those heavy, spiky metal squares and rounds at your gran's house? These are called flower frogs, or more commonly known as kenzan, and are very handy. Scan online trading platforms and second-hand shops for the originals or search online for the modern versions. They sit at the bottom of your vase (some use Plasticine to help secure them to the vase, but I mostly freestyle) and you build your arrangement by spiking stems into their centres.

Another fantastic, liberating option is chicken wire. I prefer the coated type and roughly cut up a square of it, guesstimating around one and a half times the size of vessel it needs to fill. I then crudely curl it over to create a pillow form and push inside the vessel. This acts as a reusable and super effective support for stems in all manner of vases. If you are dealing with longer, heavier stems you would want to add some extra support by crisscrossing the rim of the vase with florist's pot tape. This is a skinny, very sticky tape that you can easily procure online. However, mostly I find that the chicken wire can be jammed pretty well into the vases if the top is narrower than the base.

Previous page: Freshly cut stems having a good drink before being arranged – sweet peas, bearded iris, hosta leaves, renga renga, aquilegia and purple toadflax.
Left: My growing collection of vases, predominantly second-hand finds.
Above: Top row: Curling cut coated chicken wire snuggly into a vessel to act as a support for stems. **Middle row:** A small flower frog (also known as a kenzan) is gently dropped into a small vase ready for stems to be spiked into it. **Bottom row:** A pillow of coated chicken wire is secured further in a wide-necked vessel by crisscrossing the opening with florist specific pot tape.

Arranging flowers is an uncomplicated activity that offers a reprieve in a busy day and a distraction for a busy mind. The growing of 'soul food' as opposed to actual 'food', is of different but worthy value to your wellbeing.

Left: *Verbena bonariensis* and *Verbena rigida* mixed in with 'Iceberg' roses, sweet peas, honeysuckle, purple toadflax and foxgloves.

TIPS FOR HARVESTING

When picking it is often easier to use finer-nosed snips or even scissors as opposed to secateurs which are heavier and harder to be precise. It's best to pick in the morning or evening, outside the heat of the day to give your flowers the best chance of survival. When harvesting blooms you are aiming to select for optimum potential of vase life. Consider the length of stem and cut in a way that encourages your plant to keep flowering. To be honest, sometimes you just have to take what you can get and short stems with overly mature blooms might just have to be it! As plants move through their seasonal life cycle, flowering stems seem to get shorter, so don't stress, just make cuter posies.

In most situations choosing blooms that have opened about a third to a half, with the remainder still in bud will give you an advantage to lasting longer in a vase, particularly true for foxgloves, delphiniums and snapdragons. Once flowers have been visited by pollinators their vase life is greatly reduced. Others need to be newly, but fully open with mature colour and strong stems rather than floppy, juvenile ones – relevant for many plants like dahlias, cosmos and also umbellifers like fennel and Queen Anne's lace.

Once you have chosen your flowering stem, slide your snips down to where it meets the main stem and make a clean cut. It's in this little intersection that many flowering plants will be encouraged to generate new growth, equalling renewed display for your garden and another round of potentials for the vase.

For diligent harvesting practice you can scout the garden with a half-filled bucket of water to give instant relief for flowers while in transit.

CONDITIONING

As soon as you have picked, pop your bunch of stems promptly into a jug or sink of water to keep them happy. They love it right up to their necks if possible. Some plants are sulky and give you a very short window after cutting before they will start to irretrievably wilt if not plunged into water quickly.

Before you set up your vase, whip through the stems and condition them ready for arranging by stripping and trimming all leaves, branches or thorns that you think will sit below the water line and get caught up in any supports you are using. Leaves left in the water will quickly rot and greatly limit the life of the whole arrangement.

Woody stems (like branches of blossom, hydrangeas and roses) are helped along by cutting twice. Once across the stem on a 45-degree angle, then again, around 5 cm or more vertically 'up' the stem to split it open, allowing for greater surface area to hydrate from. Other flowers (like poppies and hellebores) benefit from a quick sear in boiling water to help prevent them wilting in the vase. A 10-second dip of the bottom 5 cm of a stem before going straight into the vase of cold water can work well! You will see the dunked stem changes colour.

Left: Loading up the trusty trug with renga renga, purple toadflax, aquilegia, sweet peas, bearded iris, clematis and elder foliage.
Above: Sweet peas, geum, aquilegia flowers and foliage hydrating before arranging.

Some plants like daffodils and euphorbia are super sappy and should be handled with care, to avoid getting the sap on your skin. Cleanly snip them just once then pop into their own jug of water to allow the sap to dispel and the stem to slightly seal before including in your arrangement. The sap can be toxic to your other blooms, so this little rest period is helpful. Avoid recutting them when moving into an arrangement as this will release the sap once again.

If you are finding your favourite garden flowers are not doing well in a vase, a quick search online for cutting tips is well worth it.

Gappy, stumpy, wonky, unbalanced and battling colour palettes are a by-product of selecting from a small seasonal library of flowering plants. The results are always distinctly domestic and homely. Just the way I like it.

ARRANGING FLOWERS AT HOME

In my first few years of enthusiastic home-based flower arranging, I found building bunches in narrow-necked vessels like old milk bottles a little easier to get going. As I discovered that playing around with my produce was akin to meditation, I became keener to experiment with size and flower type. I have found great inspiration from books like *A Year in Flowers* by iconic Erin Benzakein of Floret Farm in the USA, *A Tree in the House* by the fantastically creative Annabelle Hickson and the IGTV and online floristry course of UK's Willow Crossley. I honestly find these better than the Headspace app.

For me, playing around with the display of flowers comes only second to growing them in my garden. It's creativity for the sake of it, existing in peace behind my own front door and turning a blind eye to standards upheld by those making a living selling their creations. It's fun to know the basics and mechanics but mostly only to then break them as I am my only client and I choose to be extremely non-judgemental.

Gappy, stumpy, wonky, unbalanced and battling colour palettes are a by-product of selecting from a small, seasonal library of flowering plants and the results are always distinctly domestic and homely. Just the way I like it.

Left to right: Searing the bottom of some plant stalks in just boiled water helps them last longer in the vase; before arranging stems, strip all the foliage from the stalks that will sit below the water line of the vase; a large, entirely foraged late spring arrangement collected from the Christchurch residential red zone. Featuring 'Sally Holmes' rose, lupins, common yarrow, vetch, cat's ears, honeysuckle, tree lupins, forget-me-nots and a few mystery roses. All supported in silver wine bucket with a large flower frog inside it.

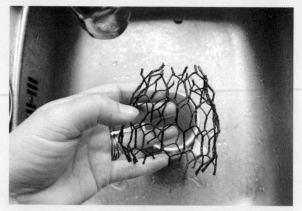

BUILDING AN ARRANGEMENT

To encourage you to start arranging your own flowers indoors I would recommend these simple tips:

• Before you start building your arrangement, consider where it will sit in your space. Does it need to be viewed from all angles on the kitchen table? Or will it sit with its back against a wall? This immediately gives you cues on how to construct it, ensuring the focal point is on full display.

• Don't forget foliage. Use it to firstly map out the vague shape and height that you would like to see for your completed arrangement. Consider an asymmetry outline for a casual look including some of your shorter stems swooping around the lip of the vase.

• Alternatively, you could begin your arrangement by working from the outer rim of your vessel, beginning with shorter stems and working towards the centre for the taller and to highlight your hero bloom/s.

• Aim for your arrangements to be around 1–2 times the height of your vessel for a comfortable scale. Reduce your vase size to work with shorter stems.

• Work with the natural bend and wonkiness of stems, testing which way they want to point in the vase instead of forcing them into submission. You will lose!

• Backfill with your variety of blooms, staggering heights and scattering to balance, doing your best with the lengths and quantity you can afford from your garden. Don't seek out perfection!

• As an amateur arranger limited to your garden's offering on any given day, it is not always easy to have a showstopping hero bloom or three for each posy like you will often see in beautiful professional bunches. Just gather everything you can get your hands on and have a play. The making is the therapeutic bit!

• Alternatively, consider buying a bunch of exciting store-bought blooms to then add to your home-grown mixed arrangements. It's best to seek out New Zealand-grown in these cases rather than out-of-season imports. Flower farming is gaining popularity so explore any direct-from-farmgate sales in your area.

• Arrangements of a single type of flower en masse look lush but a ragtag mixed arrangement of everything flowering in your plot is equally satisfying and romantic.

• If possible, when making mixed bunches it's often best to work with uneven numbers of each bloom you are scattering through. For example, 1, 3, 5 and so forth.

• Always recut each stem by 2 cm, on a 45-degree angle before threading into your arrangement.

Pictured: A springtime bedside posy made of thalictrum, sweet peas, fennel, cornflowers, forget-me-nots, a white snapdragon and a wonky spring onion.

CARING FOR YOUR PICKED BUNCH

There are some fantastic products out there for extending the life of your arrangements – think little sachets of perkiness used by many florists. My mum has mentioned the odd dash of bleach, concoctions of aspirin or sugar can do wonders too so it's worth a google to decide for yourself.

However, for my home bunches, made quickly for our household to enjoy, I simply use fresh water in clean vases, topping up every day and changing out completely when possible every three or so days. If easily accessible, I give all the stems a fresh snip too on day three. If you have created a big heavy display, sometimes it's just too tricky to do this, so don't sweat it.

It's really common for me to dismantle a fading vase of flowers, discard the dead stems to the compost and retrim the perky ones to include in another vase. Stems of love-in-a-mist, fennel and rudbeckia often migrate from one arrangement to another, multiple times over.

Arranging your own flowers is a simple joy and each change in season brings new fodder and ideas. Be inspired by other home gardeners sharing on social media as much as your neighbour's windowsill.

Left to right: A lush bunch of foxgloves, geums, sweet peas, love-in-a-mist, astilbe, bearded iris, honeysuckle, purple toadflax and sanguisorba foliage in a Wundaire vase; slim winter pickings of hellebores, jonquils, plum blossom, snowflakes and broccolini flower in an Oka Pottery cup; it is fun to mix flash locally grown flowers in with your humble seasonal specimens. This is a large frothy arrangement of foxgloves, fennel, honeysuckle, aquilegia, love-in-a-mist, sweet peas, bearded iris, 'Iceberg' roses, purple toadflax, nasturtium foliage and a single Iceland poppy playing tribute to lush ranunculus from Verve Flowers in Marlborough.

Glossary

Annual
A plant that will grow, flower, set seed and die in a single year.

Aphids
Tiny green insects that mass on leaves and buds of plants, sucking on their nutrients.

Biennial
A plant that completes its life cycle over two years. From germination of seed, establishing roots, stems and leaves the first year. In the second year they flower, set seed and die.

Blight
A type of fungal disease that attacks plants causing sudden yellowing, withering and dying of leaves, flowers, fruit or the entire plant.

Blood and bone
Store-bought, powdered mix of rich organic matter that encourages healthy plant growth and improves soil quality, supporting worm and soil microbe activity.

Bloom ('to bloom'/'blooming')
Another nice name for a flower.

Bud
The enclosed, compact growth stage before developing into a flower, stem or leaf.

Bulbs/Corms/Tubers/Rhizomes
Storage organs that various perennial plants develop and grow from. Each with unique needs for planting.

Clump/Clump-forming
Referring to the dense, underground root base created by perennial plants as they mature.

Coated chicken wire
Very malleable, gridded sheets of wire purchased off the roll or in pre-packaged rolls. Coated in a smooth plastic for easy use. Is easily sectioned off into desired size when cut with secateurs or pliers. Used in this book for creating stem supports within vases.

Compost
Mixed organic matter that has broken down from its original forms to create a rich soil-like substance that when added to a garden bed, provides nutrients to aid growth. Can be made at home over time or purchased bagged.

Conditioning
The process of preparing a cut stem for the vase by hydrating in water and trimming all leaves and branches on the lower stem.

Containers
Above-ground options for planting into.

Cultivar
(Short for 'cultivated variety'), a group of plants with the same characteristics that will be maintained when propagated from root division or cutting. It is not guaranteed to produce the same when grown from seed.

Cut and come again
A category of plants that respond to deadheading and harvesting of blooms to continue to keep producing flowers for longer into the season until the first frosts, disease or natural winter decline claims them.

Cut flower
Refers to a flowering stem when cut from a plant to be used in a flower arrangement.

Cuttings
The process of propagating new plants from a piece of snipped-off growth off another.

Deadheading
The process of removing faded and spent blooms from a plant before it turns into a seed head to encourage continued production of flowers. Best done with sharp, slim-nosed garden snips, above and close to an intersection with branch, stem or leaf node.

Dividing
The process of cultivating new plants by dividing the root clump of another and replanting.

Fertiliser
A variety of organic and non-organic additives that can be added to the soil around your plant to feed it, improving health and performance. Available in a variety of forms including powders, liquids, tablets, pellets and sprays.

Flower frog
Also known as a kenzan, a heavy, metal disc topped with sharp spikes to support flower stems in a vase. Can come in a variety of sizes and shapes.

Germination
The first development of a plant from a seed.

Half-Hardy annual
An annual plant that is best started from seed undercover before planting out seedlings after the risk of frost has gone.

Hardening off
The process of placing new potted seedlings outside during the day/mild nights to acclimatise before planting out. Most useful for glasshouse-raised seedlings.

Hardy annual
An annual plant that can be sown directly in the ground where you want them to grow and is tolerant of cold and frosts.

Hybrid
A plant created by crossbreeding two differing species or varieties.

Irrigation
A water delivery system, either fixed or mobile.

Legionnaires' disease
A dangerous form of atypical pneumonia caused by a legionella bacteria. This is commonly found in freshly opened bagged soil, compost, potting mix and mulch, exposing a person if breathed in while dry. A mask and gloves is the first line of defence, as is wetting mix before use.

Mites
Tiny insects that can take up residence to feed on plants, reducing their performance or sometimes killing them. There are many species that are attracted to particular plants.

Mulch
A layer of organic or inorganic matter spread on surface of garden beds, around plants. To aid in reducing weeds and retaining moisture.

Niwashi tool
A versatile gardening tool modelled on traditional Japanese hand trowel.

Pellets
Referring to sheep and/or chicken pellets. Chicken and sheep manure processed into easy-to-use pellets to be added to soil where they will naturally break down with moisture over time and feed the soil in your garden.

Perennial
A plant that recedes down to its roots each winter, to regrow, flower and seed again for three more years.

Permaculture
A concept of gardening based on sustainable, organic and harmonious cycles observed in nature.

Pinching
The process of snipping off the central growing stem between a pair of side stems or leaves to promote bushier, stronger growth and more flowers.

Plant food
A common name for a multitude of options to fertilise and encourage healthy growth of a plant. To 'feed' a plant refers to fertilising it.

Plant type
Referring to the categories and sub categories of plants falling under perennial, annual and biennial.

Planting out
The process of moving established seedlings from pots to the garden.

Pollinator
Referring to bees and other insects that aid in the fertilisation by transporting 'male' pollen grains to meet the 'female' stigma in another flower to allow plants to create seeds.

Pot tape
Tape coming in a variety of widths that has strength when stretched and secured across the top of a vessel. Useful for creating extra support to hold down pillows of chicken wire in wide-rimmed vessels used for flower arranging. Easily ordered online in florist supply stores.

Potting mix
Store-bought, bagged organic matter that has been specifically improved with added nutrients to provide plants with productive conditions for growing in a container.

Potting on
The process of moving new small seedlings into a larger pot to continue growing undercover.

Powdery mildew
A common fungal disease that develops on plants, appearing as a filmy white powder on their leaves. Triggered by the stress of a plant being underwatered, too densely planted or too much moisture overnight.

Pricking out
The process of gently prizing tiny new seedlings out of their pot.

Propagation
The process of creating new plants.

Propagator
A mini, table-top glasshouse designed to germinate and raise seedlings in, offering a water delivery system and clear lid to create a humid atmosphere.

Pruning
Mostly refers to the end-of-season cutting back of spent growth on perennial plants, roses and hydrangeas to aid in fresh new growth the following spring. Also refers to the manual shaping and tidying of trees and shrubs using secateurs, long-handled pruners or hedge trimmers.

Punnet
A small seed tray or vessel, mostly made of plastic, that is used to raise seeds in.

Root cutting
The process of propagating new plants from a separated root of another.

Runner
A long horizontal stem shooting out from the base of a plant, that allows new plants to form along its length.

Rust
A common fungal disease that presents as rust-coloured spots on the leaves of many plants such as roses, snapdragons, geraniums and hollyhocks. Often occurring due to prolonged dampness and humidity.

Secateurs
Strong, plant-specific garden scissors.

Seed head
The final stage of a plant's cycle when a pollinated flower loses its petals to present its seeds instead.

Seed raising
The process of germinating seeds and fostering their seedlings in a controlled, undercover environment.

Seed tray
A plastic or biodegradable moulded tray with capsules to fill with seed mix to germinate seeds and raise seedlings undercover.

Self-seed
Some plants produce seeds that eagerly germinate and produce new plants, naturally spreading to the ground around the original.

Shoot
A fresh young stem emerging from the ground toward light.

Shrubs
Perennial plants that are smaller than trees and have woody stems above the ground when dormant.

Sow
The process of placing seeds in seed mix or garden to prepare for germination and growth.

Spacing
The recommended distance for planting or sowing a seed from neighbouring plants.

Species
A group classification of plants sharing similar traits and appearance.

Staking
Supporting delicate, tall plants with heavy blooms to avoid collapsing. Long stakes or circular supports made from wood or metal are commonly used.

Teepee
A cone-shaped structure made from lengths of wood for plants to grow up.

Tender perennial
Perennial plants that are intolerant of exposure to cold temperatures and frosts, causing them to die.

Toxicity
In gardening refers to potential of a plant to poison humans or animals

Trowel
A small handheld spade.

Trug
A handy long and shallow basket with handles suitable for transporting harvested vegetables and flowers.

Tuber rot
A spreading decay of a tuber caused by bacteria triggered by soggy conditions, over-fertilising and overcrowding.

Umbellifer
Plants with umbrella-shaped floral display.

Underplant
The process of layering planting by positioning shorter plants below taller ones.

Variety
A group of plants within a species with similar characteristics that will produce 'true-to-seed'. Can be found growing consistently the same in nature.

Woody base
Refers to the strong, wood-like stems created by some plants as they reach maturity.

Below: Casual sprigs of
marjoram in the afternoon
sun of my office. Print by
Maddy Young.

Thank you

Tonia Shuttleworth, you are the best creative partner I could have ever hoped to find. Thank you so much for recognising my vision for this book, adopting it as your own and making it better than I could have ever imagined. Your calm approach and passion for your business promises an incredible future for Koa Press. I am incredibly honoured to be your debut book.

To Lucinda Diack, you are my literary fairy godmother! I shudder to think what any other editor would have done with my wayward, casual words and I have so much respect for your light touch and constant reassuring guidance.

To Belinda O'Keefe, I breathed a sigh of relief every time a proof came back with botanically correct titles and your fact checking all saved us from at least one embarrassing mistake!

To Penny Zino of 'Flaxmere', Carolyn Ferraby of 'Barewood' and the other incredibly generous and knowledgeable gardeners above me. Your unwavering enthusiasm for my ideas, despite my lack of experience, gave me the confidence to bring this book to life.

To my family, you've always offered a supportive hand to all of my projects. It's really nice to have one cemented in print that we can all share. Also to my dog/cat Tonka, never leaving me to walk the garden edges alone and sunbathing on top of baby seedlings without fail.

To my husband T, constantly wading through waves of fallen petals on the kitchen bench and a hay fever induced haze with each new arrangement that arrives inside. Your relentless support and time spent out there with me means there would of course be no garden, let alone a book, without you. There are never enough words to express my love for you.